# The Vegetarian Italian Kitchen

# The Vegetarian Italian Kitchen

### Veronica Lavenia

NEW
HOLLAND

To Stefania

*I like the food not ordered many days before, nor served by the hands of many, simple and easy to find. A food that has nothing sophisticated or precious that will not fail anywhere you go, not expensive for shareholders, nor for the body.*

Plato

# CONTENTS

# An Italian Kitchen Garden Under The Volcano

I was born and grew up surrounded by nature and good food, on the slopes of Mount Etna, in Sicily.

In this stunning land of myths and legends, fire, water and light come together in a show of nature that has no equal in its kind. Among the lava rocks grows one of the most valuable pistachios (PDO) in the world, it is called 'green gold'. Its color is as unique as its intense flavor – a deep emerald green with purple tints.

In the rich valley between Noto to Avola some of the finest varieties of almonds are cultivated. It is no coincidence that dried fruits (pistachio and almonds, in particular), are the undisputed heroes of Sicilian cuisine, and have been since the time of Arab domination.

Prickly pears (Indian figs) give life to juicy fruits, and make delicious jams, while the honey from the Ape Nera (Slow Food Presidium Sicilian black bees), grown in areas around Mount Etna, is the main ingredient of many Sicilian sweets.

Vines and olive groves further enrich this valuable culinary heritage. Blood oranges and lemons scent the Sicilian countryside, reminding us that nature has provided us with the best food for healthy eating.

In such varied soil, full of gastronomic delights, it is not difficult to distinguish real food from 'everything else'.

Accustomed to the rich flavors of the garden cultivated by my father, I learnt as a child to recognize the beauty and the goodness of vegetables grown without fertilizers, distinct from flavorless industrial-grown ones. It was a little garden, but in every season we found vegetables we loved. And with these precious jewels of nature my mother made luscious, healthy meals. A habit that continues today and that, inevitably, I have inherited.

That's the charm of Italian cuisine: the luxury of simplicity.

I was lucky enough to take snacks to school that were prepared by my mother and shop bought temptations were the exception and not the rule for me (although, like many kids, I was attracted by them). This was an advantage that enabled me, growing up, not to enslave my palate to fake flavors of prepackaged food. Of course, once grown, and often being away from home for study and work, I had to adapt to the circumstances, but I always avoided, as far as possible, foods that didn't nourish.

Nourish. This is a privilege of home cooking. An important commitment, a value to grow now more than ever, in a society that runs fast, distracted by form and not drawn to substance.

It happens, sometimes, that the words 'Eat' and 'Feed' are interchanged. In truth, the difference between them is substantial. 'Eating' involves taking food to appease hunger. 'Feeding', however, means providing our body with the substances they need in the right amounts. This involves learning a conscious and balanced way of eating, which doesn't sacrifice the pleasure of sitting around a table and, on the contrary, enhances the beauty of the products that nature offers us. It is not a sterile, boring 'back to basics' way of eating but a very simple way to seek what is best for us. And the best ingredients can be affordable for everyone. You just need to know what to choose. Simple is better. Less is more. These rules are timeless, important in life as well as in cuisine, especially when it comes to Italian food.

For Italians, eating is not only what goes in your mouth, but also how you eat. It means taking care of the people we love, sitting down and taking your time. Time to feed, to enjoy the small pleasures of life, time to share.

We live in a time where fads come quickly and then, just as fast, disappear. Food is not excluded from these cycles. The so called 'superfood' is ubiquitous and, it seems, irreplaceable. Centenarians living in some small towns of southern Italy have reached this enviable goal without knowing what 'superfoods' are but passing on, within their families, recipe notebooks, the result of centuries-old traditions. They are tangible evidence that 'diet' is a lifestyle, not a trend or, worse, calorie control.

The Mediterranean diet has remained unchanged for centuries, the subject of numerous scientific studies that all come to the same conclusion: minimalism is true wealth. Vegetables, whole grains, legumes and fruit enrich the recipes in this book. Healthy true Italian dishes, made with unrefined ingredients (now readily available in supermarkets and organic food stores), show that traditions endure.

This book is a collection of tasty Italian ideas (with a look at meat substitutes like tofu and seitan, ingredients not belonging to Italian tradition but, by now, firmly entered into Italian vegetarian and vegan restaurant menus), regularly enjoyed by me and the people I love. It celebrates food in its purest form.

*Veronica*

# My Natural Pantry

The pantry of our grandmothers was the most simple and healthy that could exist; a magic chest from which they pulled out the best that nature put at their disposal. Every season had its flavors and our grandmothers were the best nutritionists.

Today, the consumer needs specific skills. Otherwise, the risk is not to know what and how much exists in many foods (we're talking tropical oils, added sugars, preservatives, additives, refined flours etc.).

Modern food is beautiful and inviting but much less healthy and tasty than it once was. But we are not powerless in the face of a certain type of market. We can make a difference. We can choose whether to buy this or that product, but to do so we need to know. Knowledge is the only means by which we consumers can affect the laws of the market. Emphasis should be placed not only on 'healthy recipes' but also on organic unrefined ingredients.

Waiting for the arrival of a new season, with the colors and scents of its products, is one of those simple emotions that must be safe-guarded. Until a few decades ago, eating only seasonal ingredients was the norm, while today, often, is the exception. We can have everything at any time.

The primary aim of contemporary industries is to satisfy every desire of the consumer. This has made us lazy, spoilt and, above all, impatient. The beauty of fruit and vegetables lies in being cultivated, and as far as possible, respecting the health of human beings and our planet. We let ourselves be seduced by appearances – ignoring the quality of a seasonal fruit that maybe a bit bruised, is a weakness that doesn't help our well-being or even our wallets.

Preferring seasonal fruit and vegetables means to pander to the rhythms of nature, you can also enjoy fresh sustainable food that tastes real at a cheaper price.

The next step, when possible, is to choose organic fruit and vegetables. This allows you to enjoy all their flavor and, above all, to get your fill of all the vitamins contained in the skin of many fruits such as apples, pears, peaches and apricots. Nowadays, organic fruits and vegetables are available in traditional supermarkets at good value for money. An essential rule is to read the label of everything we buy to verify the origin of the product, method of cultivation, production date and expiration date. Of course, buying directly from the farmer, when possible, is the best choice and enables you to learn more about the product.

Many vegetables used for my recipes are from my family garden. When the garden is not enough I buy from farmers. The list of fruits and vegetables below is not exhaustive, of course, but it refers to many of the products used in the preparation of my recipes that are easily available. You can integrate them, depending on your country of origin, with local fruits and vegetables.

I prefer to steam cook my vegetables (unless a recipe requires another type of cooking). This method is recommended as the vegetables retain their nutrients and their flavor is better.

If consumed daily, the precious beneficial properties of fruit and vegetables are ideal allies for your wellness. To make the most of these benefits, you should retain them properly, as I suggest below.

## VEGETABLES

### Artichokes:

Artichokes have a diuretic, antioxidant, protective and liver stimulant effect. To keep them in the freezer, you have to remove the harsh outer leaves. Holding them vertically, squash them gently between the palms of your hands, so as to open them a little which will allow the water to better penetrate them. Soak them in water and lemon juice for at least half an hour so that they don't oxidize. Boil a large pot of water and lemon juice and let the artichokes cook for two minutes. Drain and place them on a plate, upside down, to dry and cool completely. Once cold and dry, put the preserved artichokes in a container and freeze. Artichokes prepared like this are ready to be cooked without being thawed.

### Asparagus:

A source of vitamin A, B, C and E, asparagus strengthens the immune system, fights fatigue and has a detoxifying, purifying and draining action. To test their freshness at the time of purchase, the shoots must be firm, a bright color and with closed tops because, if they are open, the asparagus is old. To eat them, you have to remove the woody ends. They should be stored in the refrigerator, wrapped in a damp cloth.

## Broccoli and cauliflower:

Broccoli and cauliflower have many properties in common. One of these key properties is their anti-cancer action. They are also excellent in the fight against cholesterol, thanks to the high concentration of calcium and vitamin K.

Raw and unwashed, broccoli and cauliflower can be stored in the refrigerator for up to ten days, but once cooked you can keep them for a maximum of two days. Remember, though, that the longer you keep them the more their characteristic odor increases.

Being delicate vegetables, and therefore perishable, both should be used fresh, this also allows you to benefit fully from their properties. Before freezing, steam the florets of broccoli and cauliflower for three minutes.

## Capers:

Capers are a symbol of traditional Sicilian food. The best known are the capers of Pantelleria Island (Western Sicily) and the Aeolian Islands (Eastern Sicily).

The consumption of capers is helpful for protecting blood vessels. They contain vitamins A, B and C and are rich in minerals such as calcium, potassium, iron and phosphorus. Real Sicilian capers are preserved in salt and, if well conserved, they can last for years.

## Carrots:

Carrots are rich in minerals such as iron, calcium, magnesium, potassium, copper and zinc; vitamins A,B and C; and beta-carotene. Carrots should be stored in the refrigerator in a plastic bag. If purchased with the tops, cut the carrots off before storing in the refrigerator, otherwise the leaves deteriorating will contribute to the deterioration of the carrots themselves.

## Celery:

Known for its purifying properties, antidepressant and calming qualities, celery is a source of phosphorus, calcium, iron, vitamins C and B, and also has beneficial effects on blood pressure. Used for the preparation of sauces (with carrot and onion), it is also a key ingredient for vegetable broths, soups and salads. You can consume raw celery (after removing the filaments) as a great breakfast.

## Eggplant (Aubergine):

Very rich in minerals, especially potassium, phosphorus and magnesium, the eggplant also contains vitamin A, B, C and K, and a high concentration of water.

## Fennel:

It is an excellent diuretic and digestive, rich in minerals such as potassium, calcium, phosphorus, sodium, magnesium, iron, zinc, manganese, selenium and vitamins A, B and C. It should be kept in the refrigerator in a plastic bag with holes and must be consumed in the short term. It can also be frozen, after cutting it into pieces and blanching for 4–5 minutes. Let cool before freezing in the water it was blanched in.

## Garlic:

It regulates blood pressure and, like onion, is a natural antibiotic. It helps to lower the levels of cholesterol and triglycerides in the blood.

To clean your breath of garlic after a meal just chew a sage leaf, a mint leaf, a coffee bean or the seeds of star anise.

To mitigate the strong smell of garlic it is preferable to use the cloved garlic coated with its 'skin'.

As with potatoes, the ideal storage temperature to avoid sprouts is 10°C (50°F). The garlic should be stored protected from light and, once opened, can be sliced (or crushed) and kept in the freezer for several months inside a container or a freezer bag for food.

## Green beans:

They are a source of minerals, particularly potassium, iron, calcium, vitamin A and protein. For storage in the freezer it is advisable to check the two ends, blanch for two minutes, cool and then freeze. At the moment of their use, cook in boiling water for seven minutes. To keep their bright green color, cook in plenty of water and salt in an uncovered pot, at a fast boil, for a few minutes. Leaving the pot uncovered is essential to make sure that the acids present in beans evaporate before attacking the chlorophyll.

## Leek:

Rich in vitamin A and minerals like iron, magnesium, potassium and calcium. As is always better, consume this fresh vegetables in the shortest possible time. To preserve the leek for longer, after cleaning, just blanch it for a few minutes (avoid cutting it and storing raw because it tends to oxidize) and store in appropriate freezer bags.

## Lettuce:
Able to adapt to any type of climate, this vegetable grows well even at low temperatures. For this reason, and thanks to its cultivation it is an excellent food available throughout the year in many varieties (iceberg, butter head, leaf and romaine). It is a source of iron, calcium, phosphorus, copper, sodium, potassium, vitamins A and C.

A good quality lettuce must have a hard clump, be well closed, with healthy and tender leaves and bright colors. Once purchased, place the lettuce in a container covered with a damp cloth and place in a drawer of the refrigerator where the air can circulate. Lettuce can be kept for a maximum of 3–4 days.

## Onion:
It is a natural antibiotic, has a stimulating action, is diuretic and purifying and facilitates blood circulation. The proper storage of onions is crucial to avoid sprouting. It is advisable to keep the onions in a wicker basket, covered with sheets of paper, inside a cardboard box or a paper bag. If you have picked the onions from your vegetable garden, leave them to stand in the air but away from direct sunlight, placing them on sheets of newspaper. Once you open an onion, the remaining part can be sliced or diced and frozen for future use. The onion can also be kept open for two or three days in the refrigerator inside the fruit and vegetable tray.

## Parsley:
An indispensable ingredient in Italian cuisine, a good source of vitamin A, B and K, parsley is useful for bone health, for its action in the clotting of blood, for eyesight and the immune system.

## Peas:
Rich in vitamin C, folic acid and vitamin B6, peas are allies of the cardiovascular system and help to maintain low cholesterol levels. When you buy fresh peas (always preferable to frozen ones) the shell should appear bright and not yellow. Once purchased, you can keep them in the fridge for a few days, they should be peeled

because the skin of the fruit tends to harden easily.

## Capsicum (bell pepper):
It contains a very high percentage of vitamin C, is rich in phosphorus, magnesium, potassium, iron and calcium. Capsicum is also a source of vitamins B, E, J, K and potassium, and has the presence of vitamin A.

## Potatoes:
They are a useful help against hypertension, rich in vitamin C and potassium. Potatoes should be stored correctly to prevent sprouting and green spots. These two features indicate an increase in the concentration of solanine, a substance which, when accumulated excessively by the body, can be toxic.

## Pumpkin:
They are rich in beta-carotene (as with all orange plants) and antioxidants useful for regenerating cells. When purchasing, the pumpkin should be heavy, the skin should be clean and free from bruises. A whole pumpkin, can be stored all winter in a dark, cool and dry environment. Pieces of pumpkin, should be preserved in the refrigerator, wrapped in transparent paper (in this case it should also be eaten within a few days). If, instead, you want to keep in the freezer, you must first remove the peel, cut the pumpkin into cubes and blanch it for a few minutes.

## Radicchio:
Also called red chicory, it is derived from wild chicory which keeps its bitter taste. The crunchy radicchio leaves are one of the main ingredients of Italian cuisine, especially in the preparation of salads. 'Round Radicchio from Chioggia' is the most common and cheapest (the most prized is the 'Radicchio from Treviso'), available almost all year round. Upon purchase, the leaves should not be wilting or too wet. It can be eaten both raw and cooked. Before use and after washing thoroughly, open the leaves well and soak in cold water for about 15 minutes to mitigate the bitter taste. The typical bitter taste gives the radicchio purifying, tonic and laxative effects, facilitating digestion and diuresis. Anthocyanins, substances that give the leaves their red color, are important due to their antioxidant and anti-inflammatory properties.

## Spinach:

A high source of iron, spinach also has a high content of vitamin A, B, D, C, F, P and K. Rich in fiber, minerals and folic acid, it is useful for eye health and for the immune system. In the supermarket, you can find organic spinach ready washed and cleaned in a bag,but it is advisable to buy it fresh. Raw spinach will keep for a few days wrapped in a clean, damp cloth. Once cooked, on the contrary, it must be consumed immediately. Fresh spinach should be washed thoroughly just before cooking (if left to soak it loses many of its nutrients), with many changes of water and the addition of bicarbonate. Stir the leaves, drain and change the water until it is completely free of any dirt. The juice of a lemon, added into the cooking, increases the availability of iron content in spinach.

## Tomatoes:

A staple of Italian cuisine, tomatoes are rich in vitamins and minerals. When buying, they must be free of spots or bruises and have a firm texture. They must be stored at room temperature and consumed within a few days.

## Zucchini (courgette):

Rich in minerals, zucchini are one of the most versatile vegetables. If not eaten immediately, zucchini can be frozen. Cut them, removing the ends and slice the zucchini, as desired, into rings or strips. Place them in a plastic bag in the freezer and freeze.

# HERBS

They are the basis of the Mediterranean cuisine. In southern Italian houses, aided by the generous climate, herbs never fail, both in the garden and on balconies. Keeping your favorite herbs at home also helps your mood, because of their beauty and lively scents. They enhance the flavor and aroma of dishes and act as the best natural antioxidant.

## Basil:

From the Latin *Basilicum*, the 'royal herb', basil is a plant known since ancient times for its valuable properties. It stimulates the appetite, is calming, an antispasmodic and fights nervousness and insomnia. After the season, you can freeze the leaves. Rinse them in cold water and dry one by one. Place the basil leaves in bags for and freeze.

## Oregano:

It contains minerals, especially iron and calcium, and vitamins C and A. During the summer, you can eat it fresh. Dried oregano, however, can be consumed all year round and is one of the most used condiments in southern Italian cuisine.

## Rosemary:

It is considered the balsamic plant par excellence, known and used since ancient times for its medicinal properties. Very rich in essential oils, in Italy it is especially used for baking recipes because its oils and fragrance seasoned the bread naturally with taste.

## Sage:

The term 'salvia' comes from the Latin *salus*, meaning health. Sage has digestive and balsamic properties. In Italy, it is used to flavor dishes, especially in winter recipes. Pasta with butter and sage is one of the most loved recipes from Italy.

# FRUIT

## Apple:

Apple is a real natural medication. If eaten raw, apple is an excellent astringent while, if eaten cooked, it helps against constipation. Rich in pectin, a substance that keeps blood sugar levels under control, it lowers dangerous cholesterol (LDL), increases the production of good cholesterol (HDL), absorbs toxins in the intestine and eliminates them.

## Apricots:

Apricots contain vitamin B and, to a lesser extent, vitamin C. Like carrots, they are rich in carotene which is effective for anti-cancer. Rich in potassium and iron they are also a source of cobalt and copper, which are useful to combat anemia.

## Bananas:

For their high content of potassium, bananas help reduce hypertension. Rich in B vitamins, including B2, which facilitates the elimination of toxins, bananas also have a good amount of iron.

## Blueberries and blackberries:

Blueberries contain many acids, in particular citric acid, which protects the cells. Also rich in folic acid, they contain high amounts of anthocyanins that strengthen the connective tissue, improving elasticity, muscle tone and eyesight. Like all berries, blackberries also contain anthocyanins, flavonoids, folic acid and are rich in vitamin C and A.

## Citrus fruits:

Citrus fruits are a rich source of vitamin C, ideal for strengthening the immune system and helping to absorb iron. They have a positive impact on the production of collagen.

Oranges provide vitamin C, pectin, soluble fiber, flavonoids and antioxidants. Moreover, they rearrange the digestive function, increasing resistance to infection.

Mandarins are a source of protein, water, vitamin B, vitamin C, magnesium, phosphorus and calcium. They contain more pro-vitamin A than any other citrus fruit and more selenium than any other type of fruit.

Lemons have vitamin C, beta-carotene and B vitamins. They also remove fat, some toxins from the blood and help for proper digestion and to improve functionality in the liver. .

Grapefruits provide potassium, vitamin D and flavonoids. A diet rich in grapefruit improves the lungs and stomach. Treatment with grapefruit also helps in cases of arthritis, kidney disease, gout, gastritis and excess uric acid.

## Peaches:
Peaches favor the elimination of toxins, aid digestion and blood circulation. They have diuretic properties, and are useful for those suffering from constipation, kidney or urinary stones.

## Pears:
Rich in calcium and potassium, which help maintain healthy bones and joints, pears are a source of vitamins B1 and B2 and, therefore, protect the skin from aging and improve life, thanks to the presence of vitamin A.

## Strawberries:
They have very high antioxidants, are rich in vitamin C, calcium, iron and magnesium. Salicylic acid contained in them helps to keep the pressure and flow of blood under control.

## Kiwis:
They have a very high content of vitamin C, higher, even than lemons, oranges and capsicum (bell peppers). Rich in potassium, vitamin E, copper and iron, kiwis help in cases of anemia and weakness of the body. The presence of calcium and phosphorus, has a protective effect on the bones, preventing and fighting osteoporosis.

## Dried fruits:
Dried fruit is a source of essential nutrients, protein, minerals, fatty acids and amino acids. Almonds and walnuts are rich in oleic acid and linoleic acid which helps reduce bad cholesterol and increase the good one. Almonds are rich in magnesium, calcium, potassium and are a good source of vitamin E and vitamin B2. When buying raisins, apricots, prunes and cranberries, check that among the ingredients there is no sulfur dioxide (used as a preservative), added sugars or tropical oils. In organic

dried fruits usually only sunflower oil is present (even better if it is cold pressed).

## CEREALS AND LEGUMES

These are staples of the Mediterranean diet. A diet rich in cereals and legumes (along with vegetables and fruit) protects the appearance of numerous widespread diseases and it is one of the tastiest ways to get your fill of energy.

### Cereals:

Cereals are herbaceous plants from the fruits of which can be derived flour. The most common are: corn; wheat; farro (in temperate regions of the planet, such as Italy); rice; barley; sorghum and millet; oats and rye. The primary characteristic of cereals is to provide 'slow-release' energy which gives the body a sense of prolonged satiety. Rich in minerals, complex carbohydrates, protein and vitamins, their cultivation dates back to prehistoric times.

Of course, the nutrients and benefits refer only to unrefined, organic, wholegrains. The fiber taken by eating wholegrains (preferably in grain form) promotes good digestive function and the soluble part of the fiber is an excellent food for the intestinal flora.

Rice and farro are the two traditional Italian foods most loved and cultivated.

### Rice:

Brown rice contains the highest value of B vitamins. Rice in general contains all the substances necessary for the human body: minerals, carbohydrates, enzymes, vitamins, proteins and fats.

### Farro:

Farro has nutritional properties superior to those of other cereals. What makes Farro so special and healthy is its characteristic to adapt to low temperatures and poor soils without the need for chemical fertilizers. Therefore, it is a natural organic food. Compared to other cereals, it also has high fiber content, low-fat and a low glycemic index. Rich in vitamins A and B, phosphorus, magnesium and potassium, Farro is rich in vegetable protein.

Legumes:

Together with cereals, legumes are able to cover your total daily protein requirement. Their cultivation is so ancient that these seeds have been found in Egyptian tombs. Legumes are the edible seeds of plants belonging to the legume family. They can be eaten fresh, dried, frozen and are easily stored. The legumes most used in Italy are: beans, peas, lentils and chickpeas. Fresh legumes are immature seeds, with a high water content, whose nutritional characteristics make them fall within the group of vegetables. Dried legumes are an excellent source of protein.

Legumes are cheap and fairtrade foods. In fact, they can be used in place of meats providing a natural and economic resource. The energy required to produce meat is ten times greater than that required to produce vegetable proteins.

Chickpeas are the most digestible legumes. Chickpea flour is used in the preparation of varied and original dishes: in Sicily, for example, it is used for the preparation of 'Panelle'; and in Liguria, for the preparation of 'Farinata'.

Beans are rich in fiber. There are more than 300 varieties, including the Italian borlotti, cannellini and dall'occhio (cowpea). Very valuable are the sorana and zolfini beans from Tuscany.

Lentils, amongst legumes, are the fastest cooking because there is no need to pre soak them. They are rich in starch and have a good iron content. There are several Italian varieties, the most notable are: Ustica lentils, from Sicily; the Altamura green lentil of Altamura, Puglia; Villalba lentils from Sicily; Fucino lentils from Abruzzo; and Castelluccio di Norcia lentils from Umbria.

## EXTRA VIRGIN OLIVE OIL

I have written extensively about the benefits and characteristics of extra virgin olive oil in my book *The Rustic Italian Bakery*. To understand how healthy it is compared to any other type of oil, is useful to remember that is the only oil obtained from the pressing of a fruit without any chemical intervention. Some argue that extra virgin olive is too expensive. Often, we do not hesitate to spend money on a brand new mobile or a computer, for a dress in the latest fad or good oil to run our car better, but we find it hard to do the same when it comes to choosing what is best for our health. It's true, a good olive oil has a high price (due to the costs of harvesting, plowing, pruning, fertilization, irrigation, transformation) but the result in terms of benefits and taste is guaranteed. True extra virgin olive oil in a bottle has a packaging that acts as a business card. Choose oils packaged in dark bottles or covered with gold paper as this protects against deterioration caused by excessive exposure to light. A cheaper alternative is cold-pressed sunflower oil, if possible organic.

## PLANT BASED DRINKS

For some they are just a fad of the moment, for others they are an alternative to dairy milk. Whatever your position on the issue, the choice is very wide. The most common plant based drinks are rice, oat, soy and almond. The lightest and most digestible, with a very delicate taste is rice milk, perfect for savory and sweet dishes. Of course, it is better to avoid plant-based drinks with extra ingredients such as added sugars and chemical vitamins. If your diet is varied, you will get the vitamins and everything you need from fruits, vegetables and grains.

## SWEETENERS

The sweeteners used for the recipes in this book are raw honey, raw sugar and fruit. The result is a series of beautiful, healthy and yummy recipes, tested and loved by even the most skeptical.

## PASTA: THE STAPLE OF THE ITALIAN DIET

My love for food started with a pasta dish. I watched while my mother, an excellent cook from whom I inherited the passion for cooking, prepared delicious meals. I liked to wait for the water to boil, and then, while the pasta was cooking, I stared at the pot, contemplating the luscious dish to come. Tasting the pasta to check its cooking was another inevitable rite to make sure it was al dente. The fact that my mother would take my advice on doneness, when I was only a child, meant a lot. Growing up, I realized she wanted, slowly, to involve me in the kitchen. A world that becomes, more or less indirectly, an important space for everyone because one eats each day and the 'independence' of an individual begins in being able to prepare a meal to be able to feed yourself. Tasting the pasta was a sort of initiation and has been one of my most important lessons.

*"You mustn't be distracted. You have to follow the cooking because even a minute longer can be enough to overcook pasta."* said my mother. *"If pasta is overcooked it will taste like glue and even the best seasoning will not give flavor to the dish."*

The term for the perfect pasta is 'al dente' and these are also the words that my mother often said to make sure I did not forget this first basic rule. But even before cooking, the choice of pasta can make a difference. The quality of grain (in Italy, pasta is only made with durum wheat) and water are the two most important factors by which one has to judge the excellence of the pasta. Even as a child I was used to eating organic durum wheat pasta, wholewheat pasta and/or farro pasta. As an adult, I also discovered corn, rice and buckwheat pasta, naturally gluten-free, which I appreciate for their high digestibility.

Abroad, it is customary to believe that fresh pasta is the most consumed product in Italy. In truth, it is dry pasta. Rigorously prepared with durum wheat, dried pasta, cooked al dente, and combined with not too elaborate sauces, is one of the signature dishes of the Mediterranean diet, a dish that Italians consume daily. Another common belief of foreigners, is that pasta (like pizza) makes you fat. However, many Italians eat a plate of pasta once a day and are among the least obese in the world. The key is to choose a really simple, fresh and seasonal sauce to go with it.

A centuries-old tradition:

Arabs introduced the use of dried pasta to western Sicily, although pasta had been eaten since Greek and Roman times under the name of 'Lagana', similar to the current word lasagna.

Over the centuries, the Sicilian and Liguria regions have given rise to the spread of dried pasta in Italy. Both Sicilians and Ligurians moved to the sea and had the need for supplies that lasted a long time, occupied little space and had a high energy input. The drying process in these regions has been favored by a perfect Mediterranean climate. At that time, pasta was made with semolina flour. The producer sat down on a bench and used his feet to mix and knead the dough. Naples was one of the cities that first imported pasta from Sicily and it also was the city that, in 1600, marked a turning point for the production of dried pasta (in Italian: 'Pasta secca') as a typical product of Italian culture.

In Naples, pasta was lying in the reeds exposed to sunlight or fresh air. Soon, Gragnano, a small town near Naples, became famous for its high quality pasta, thanks to perfect weather (sun, wind and the right humidity). In the past, the main streets of this small city were designed specifically to be best used for the natural drying of pasta, with special exposure to the sun. Gragnano pasta (nowadays exported all over the world and sold in supermarkets and shops of the best Italian food) is obtained by grinding the wheat grown in specially demarcated areas and reducing it to flour. Flour is mixed with water from the springs of the valley and left to lie on wooden frames. Then, the dough is cut with a knife by the 'cutters', according to the desired size and dried with advanced machinery.

Until the end of the 18th century, pasta was consumed without any seasoning or only with cheese. With the discovery of the Americas, tomatoes soon found fertile soil in the Mediterranean countries and slowly became to be used as a sauce for pasta. The first tomato sauce (with salt and basil), was invented in southern Italy to flavor 'macaroni' pasta.

Pasta is considered a complete food, with a low-calorie intake, since it is composed of highly digestible carbohydrates and a good source of iron and B vitamins. Wholewheat pasta or durum wheat pasta are the best and healthy ideas to introduce into your diet.

Pasta cooking tips:
- Pasta cooking time depends on its size and thickness. It should be cooked al

dente, not over cooked or under cooked. In this way, it is more digestible, tasty and the nutritional properties remain unchanged.

- Pasta should be cooked in a large saucepan otherwise it tends to stick during cooking.
- Add salt only when the water reaches a boil.
- The cooking water must remain clear, indicating the high quality of the grain.
- Long pasta must be submerged in the pot and it must not be broken. Stir gently, frequently for the first few minutes so that pasta does not stick and, occasionally, during the rest of the cooking.
- Each type of pasta has its own cooking time but the safest method to see if it is ready is to taste it. You can also test the hardness of pasta with a fork or by evaluating the exterior color of pasta that becomes clearer during cooking.
- When draining pasta always preserve a little of the cooking water, to be added in the case that pasta becomes too dry.
- Italian recipes are balanced and served in the right amount. Usually, the recommended portion is 80 g (3 oz) per person, a suggested ration, especially if the menu offers other dishes. If it is a single dish you can slightly increase the dose to 100 g (3½ oz).
- Choose a high quality brand, if possible. This is the first step that will make the difference. But do not rely on only the best-known brand. Always read the product information before buying it, the origin of the grain and choose only pasta made from durum wheat semolina. If you want to buy Italian pasta make sure it is really 'Made in Italy'. As an alternative to the various types of wheat, try: wholewheat pasta, high in fiber; Kamut, Farro or gluten-free pasta, such as buckwheat; rice and corn pasta.

## ITALIAN TOP-NOTCH PRODUCTS

My virtual culinary trip looking for the treasures of my country, begins in my homeland, Sicily. The deep south of which I am the daughter has influenced my cuisine – we prize extra virgin olive oil, citrus fruits, seasonal vegetables, flavors and bright colors.

In these pages is impossible to make a comprehensive list of everything there is to know and enjoy from Italy. I've chosen some products because they are still little-known abroad (like Modica chocolate and Trapani sea salt) but are a 'must' in the Italian culinary heritage; and other products (such as Parmigiano) that are well-known but with a secular history so rich they are worth describing. All the ingredients featured in this book are available in the best Italian specialty shops around the world and, most of them, also in the best supermarkets.

*** 

Modica – on the trail of Aztec chocolate:
Modica is a small town in the heart of Sicily, clinging to the rocks, the cradle of the Sicilian Baroque period. It is one of the most beautiful places in the world, from which runs two streams that give life to the river Moticano, and this is where the name of the city comes from.

Its strategic location was coveted by the various people who inhabited it before the age of Christ – Sicilians and Sicani, Swabians, Angevins, Greeks and Spaniards. Modica (like all of Sicily), preserves evidence, customs and practices of colonization. Modica had an artistic heritage of the most rich and varied in Sicily, unfortunately, it was destroyed in the earthquake of 1693. From the ruins little remained, but it was from there that Modica returned to shine with the construction of Baroque architecture, and later it was declared a UNESCO World Heritage Site.

Modica is famous for its historical ruins but, still more, as being the home to a very special chocolate.

For centuries, the artisans of this piece of land worked with raw chocolate. The chocolate consumed by the Aztecs had an ingredient of just cocoa mass (sometimes spices and, in some cases, raw sugar) and it was cold-worked. It is a unique, healthy, genuine product, with no added fat and lecithin free. The Spaniards brought, from Mexico to Europe, cocoa beans and the technique of making chocolate. During their colonization of Sicily, they settled in Modica and left this precious heritage with the locals (at the time of domination, the County of Modica was one of the largest and wealthiest of the Kingdom of Sicily). Leonardo Sciascia, renowned Sicilian writer, and author of *The Day of the Owl*, described the Modica chocolate as something of "incomparable flavor, which touches the absolute".

Modica chocolate processing has never passed into the industrial phase, retaining the craft and also preserving the authenticity and purity of ingredients. Over time, the only addition, compared to the Aztecs' recipe, is raw sugar and spices (vanilla, cinnamon, red chili). Without undergoing the step of conching and the addition of vegetable fat, the Modica chocolate has retained a unique flavor and quality.

The Aztecs prepared the chocolate by grinding cocoa beans on a tool called a metate, a curved stone resting on two transverse stands, using a special rolling pin also made from stone. The cocoa paste obtained was then mixed with spices and the whole lot was rubbed on the metate, until the mixture did not harden. Currently, the various stages of processing are carried out with the fastest and most modern machinery, unlike the past, when the processing was entirely by hand. The support surface on which the proceedings took place was made of lava stone and warmed prior to the three stages of processing, until the right degree of purification of chocolate was achieved. The color is dark,it has an intense perfume, and a rough texture due to the presence of grains of sugar. Its flavor differs from other chocolates due to the presence of various aromas of exotic spices, citrus fruit or dried fruit (even Nero D'Avola wine or sea salt) and for the special processing (at max 35–40°C (95–104°C)) that allows preservation of the organoleptic properties.

Exported all over the world, the PGI (Protected Geographical Indication) Modica chocolate can be considered a rare example of the treasures of past civilizations to keep as true valuable assets.

*** 

Pachino's tomatoes:
Pachino is a small Sicilian town, near Syracuse. Closer to Africa than Italy, it is known for its high-quality tomatoes, called simply Pachino. They are so special to the area and have a specific Protected Geographical Indication.
The trademark characteristics of these tomatoes and their flavor are caused by the

particular climatic conditions in which they are grown (a lot of sunshine even in the winter and salinity in the groundwater that used is for irrigation).

There are nine varieties of Pachino tomatoes. Among these, the most popular are:

- The Costoluto tomato is of an average size. It has a crunchy flesh and its intense flavor makes it perfect for salads. The innovative growing techniques used by local farmers have made this type of tomato inimitable outside the territory of Pachino.
- The Datterino tomato differs from other types of tomatoes for its small size and typical 'date' shape. It is very sweet and has a very thin skin with an intense bright red color. It is ideal for preparing bruschetta, salads and appetizers.
- Cuore di bue (bull's hearts tomato) has a pear-shape and is slightly ribbed. It has less seeds and a powdery and abundant flesh, characteristics that make it suitable for salads. The name comes from the shape of the heart of these fruits.
- Tomato Riccio (hedgehog) has a very red flesh, and is juicy and aromatic. It is great when eaten fresh and raw and is ideal for delicious tomato sauces.
- The Camone tomato is round and smooth and perfect for salads. Its taste is easily recognizable and has a perfect harmony between acidity and sugar.
- The Piccadilly tomato is a type of tomato known as "Bunch Red", it is slightly elongated in shape. Tasty and sweet, it is suitable for starters or as a side dish.

Exported all over the world, these tomatoes are a delight to try and will give your dishes a real taste of Italy. Your tomato Pachino salad, will not need other condiments outside of a good olive oil and a pinch of sea salt. A pasta dish with Pachinos only needs some fresh basil leaves and grated Parmigiano cheese.

* * *

Sicilian capers from Salina Island:

On the north of the Sicilian coast, is one of the most picturesque archipelagos in the world, and declared a World Heritage by UNESCO. The Aeolian archipelago, made up of seven volcanic islands (Lipari, Panarea, Salina, Stromboli, Vulcano, Filicudi and Alicudi), derives its name from Aeolus, the god of the winds. The Odyssey tells that Ulysses, returning from the Trojan War, once arrived to the Aeolian Islands and was hosted by Aeolus. The latter, moved by the story of the Greek hero, gave him a bottle in which they were held head winds to navigation. Thus, Ulysses on the way to Ithaca, just blew the sweet zephyr. However, while he was sleeping, his fellow navigators, believing that the wineskin contained treasures, opened it, releasing the winds. In a terrible storm, only Ulysses' ship was saved.

In truth, the Aeolian Islands, were born about two million years ago as underwater volcanoes and inhabited, by the end of the fifth millennium BC, by people from Sicily who settled in Lipari, Salina and Filicudi to exploit the economic resource of obsidian, a natural black, shiny glass generated by the sudden drop in temperature of the lava flow in the terminal phase of the eruptions.

On these islands, away from the noise of modern life, many Italians and foreigners have settled permanently after arriving first as tourists.

Salina has the most fertile island. Its name comes from the ancient salt used to store food and capers that, for centuries, were the wealth of the island. Rich in water, and green vineyards, it is the home of the Malvasia, a delicious sweet wine: DOC (defined since ancient times as 'the nectar of the gods'), which is obtained by the drying and subsequent crushing of the grapes produced by local vineyards. Salina is also known for its fine capers, with which the Sicilians give life to their unique tasty dishes.

In Salina, caper plants grow everywhere and are striking in their beauty. The flowers resemble orchids. In this land, the harvesting of capers is a ritual that traditionally falls to women. The slow and difficult harvest takes place from May to August, at dawn to avoid the heat of the period. Immediately after harvesting,the capers of Salina are laid out in the shade, on the terraces of houses covered by reeds, salted with dry sea salt and racked every day for ten days.

In addition to the bud (the caper in fact) you can prepare delicious recipes with the 'cucunci', the fruit of the caper plant. The Salina 'cucunci' are unique in the world because they do not have the classic round shape but are elongated. On the 6th June, Salina devotes an entire day to the celebration of the caper in bloom. The collection of capers follows paths through fascinating, magical places that can be visited with specialized guides to help you discover the culinary treasures that enrich Sicilian tables.

\* \* \*

Parmigiano: The Italian gold:
Parmigiano Reggiano, it is one of the best-loved cheeses in the world, the hero of

many dishes that make up the Italian culinary heritage. It is also one of the most imitated cheeses (the most counterfeited, sold with the name 'Parmesan') but the original Parmigiano is only made in Italy, and that's what gives the unique flavor to even a seemingly simple dish of pasta with tomato sauce.

This delicacy has very ancient origins, dating back to 1200. Quoted in the most ancient manuscripts, recipe books and various documents, Parmigiano was much loved by Napoleon Bonaparte who ate it with a dish of green beans. Alexandre Dumas, author of *The Three Musketeers*, wrote a gastronomic dictionary, devoting more than one line to the Parmigiano. His passion for the typical cheese of Parma was so great that he cooked macaroni with sauce and Parmigiano for guests.

Finally Molière, according to biographers, on his deathbed, asked for Parmigiano.

It was born between the monasteries of Parma and Reggio-Emiliain Northern Italy. Thanks to the abundance of rivers and wide pastures in this limited area of Emilia the making of this hard cheese spread, obtained through the processing of milk in large boilers. It forms a milk with a particular aroma that characterizes the cheese.

Today, Parmigiano-Reggiano is prepared just a year as it was nine centuries ago, with the same ingredients (precious milk from the area of origin, natural rennet and no additives), shape and unmistakable flavor.

Parmigiano has good nutritional properties, beginning with the high presence of calcium. It is also rich in protein, potassium, magnesium, zinc and has many vitamins, such as A, B6 and B2.

Each year, there are about 3 million Parmigiano shapes produced, and then sold in Italy and exported to 48 countries around the world.

Parmigiano is a table cheese but it also can be grated. For table consumption a general rule is to enjoy the cheese aged for a minimum of 12 months while, for grating, you should choose one seasoned for at least 24 months or more (also called extra-mature).

Often, Parmigiano pieces are packed in a vacuum, since the cheese can be kept for longer that way, however, in the refrigerator it can be kept wrapped in a plastic film.

In Italy, the economic value of Parmigiano Reggiano is so high that several Italian banks, take the product to guarantee the grant of a loan to the same producers.

\*\*\*

## Fontina cheese from Valle D'Aosta:

Its ancient origins date back to the 15th century. According to historical records, the term 'Fontina' is used as a name to indicate a plot of land. However, since the 1700s, the name is used to designate the cheese, and most likely to indicate the name of the Fontina pasture.

Fontina cheese from Valle d'Aosta (Northern Italy) is produced from the milk of a prized breed of cattle that gives it particular characteristics. It is produced during the summer months directly in the pasture. The key is the raw milk straight from the cow, it is so fresh that it does not undergo any intervention from the barn at the dairy. Without any added colorants or additives other than natural calf rennet and milk enzymes specific to Valle d'Aosta, the Fontina DOP has rules that production must follow to ensure the quality and origin of the product.

The minimum maturation of Fontina is 80 days, after which you get a semi-raw cheese, with a thin, soft crust. The flavor is sweet but can vary depending on the degree of maturation and pastures of origin. Rich in phosphorus, calcium and vitamins A and B, Fontina cheese is widely used in Italian cuisine. A typical dish from Valle D'Aosta is Fonduta fondue which is obtained by heating the cheese until you get a creamy texture.

* * *

## The sweet red onion from Tropea:

The Italian cuisine has different fragrances and flavors from the north to the south of the country. The south has a cuisine based mainly on vegetables, cereals and fish. Its flavors are more intense and spicy, strong and warm. Among the regions that have very specific ingredients, there is Calabria, the last piece of the Italian 'boot', from where ferries depart to reach Sicily. The red onion is one of the best-known products from this region, bathed in beautiful cobalt blue waters and fine sand.

Tropea is an ancient city of rare beauty, one of the most popular destinations for tourists attracted by its beautiful fine beaches, coves and cliffs but also from the old town and its stunning monuments. The history of Tropea is linked to many legends, one of which states that its founder was Hercules. Historians, however, date its foundation to Scipio Africanus. Tropea is derived from the Latin 'trophy' as Scipio, after the conquest of Carthage, wanted to create a city to pay homage to the gods for having protected him in the conquest of Carthage.

In this scenic land one of the world's finest onions is cultivated, with a protected geographical indication. From June to September, small and large markets, plus street markets throughout Italy, proudly display this jewel with a sweet taste and intense red color.

In southern Italy it is customary to hang the onions in the kitchen or to decorate balconies with the beautiful produce as they are joined together in characteristic braids. The typical red color is due to the presence of anthocyanin that abounds with benefits for our health (antiseptic, diuretic, helps with asthma, rheumatism, headaches, abscesses, hemorrhoids, prevents colds, regulates the amount of cholesterol in the blood, reduces cancer risk and prevents aging). The qualitative characteristics of this variety of onion depends on its genetic make-up and its interaction with the environment: the peculiarity of the terrain, proximity to the sea, the length of day, temperature and humidity.

Excellent used raw in summer salads, in Calabria it is also used to prepare a delicious jam to accompany cheese and used in the typical Tropea pie dish. Available in shops selling Italian specialties, my suggestion, if you have a small garden and the anticipation of a trip to Italy, is to buy the seeds and plant them to always have a fresh and seasonal product.

* * *

The ancient history of Aceto Balsamico from Modena:
Wine vinegar (Aceto di vino) is one of the condiments of excellence in Italian cuisine. After the fermentation and aging of wine and vinegar, you get Balsamic Vinegar of Modena, a typical product of Modena and Reggio Emilia (Northern Italy). The origins of balsamico are ancient and date back to Julius Caesar, who indicated it as a medicinal disinfectant of the digestive system.

The luck of balsamico began in the Renaissance period and is linked to the noble family of Este who ruled Ferrara from the 13th century until 1598. In that year, the Este family were forced to leave the city and move the family into Modena, the new capital of the Duchy. The passion of the Este for vinegars began in 1556 when, at the court of Ferrara, there were four types of vinegar listed. However, it was only from 1598, the year of the move to Modena, that the testimony relates to products closer to the Modena balsamico. Finally, in 1747 there was the first official testimony on the appearance of the adjective 'balsamic'. On this term there have been many reflections. The 'balms' are particularly odorous substances, and can provide relief and comfort to soothe pain. The therapeutic and digestive properties of vinegar were known for centuries. The combination of 'balsamic' in reference to the vinegar seems to indicate the pleasantness, subtlety and fine fragrances and flavors. The adjective was judged appropriate so that in a list of the various types of vinegar in the court of the Este in 1830, we find the specification of four qualities: the 'balsamic'; 'semi-balsamic'; the 'up' and the 'common'.

The story of balsamic does not end in the aristocratic courts but becomes the story of many Modena families who, for centuries, in their small acetaie have passed down recipes from generation to generation. The recipes are often jealously guarded and customized. In that period, there was a remarkable proliferation of 'balsamic' vinegars, the number of which was at least equal to that of their producers.

In 1796, Duke Ercole III d'Este was deposed by Napoleon Bonaparte and had to flee from Modena, bringing all the barrels and bottles with him. But some families in Modena continued to pass on this heritage and made it the pride of the land. In fact, the balsamico each family made was generally not sold. Each family produced and treasured it in their barrels and then donated them to precious people or used it to enrich the dowry of their daughters.

In 1989, the legislature decided the difference between Balsamic Vinegar of Modena and Traditional Balsamic Vinegar of Modena. The latter is the condiment that obtained, in 2000, the European acknowledgment of DOP (Protected Designation of Origin), produced exclusively in the provinces of Modena and Reggio Emilia by fermenting only Mosto Cotto aged in small barrels of wood for a minimum of 12 years.

Traditional Balsamic Vinegar of Modena requires many years of aging and aging. In this way, you get two balsamic qualities: the 'classic' (12 years of age) and 'extra old' (over 25 years).

DOP is a reward for producers and certainty for the consumer that they are buying an unaltered culture, tradition and quality of a product that is unique and its scents and flavors are sure to be enjoyed.

* * *

Sicilian sea salt:
The Sicilian sea salt, seen all along the road that leads from Trapani to Marsala is

(in Western Sicily) is one of those valuable goods that enriches dishes with special tastes of not only the island but the whole country.

The integral artisanal Trapani sea salt (Slow Food Presidium and IGP) is grown in a natural habitat of great charm and beauty: the WWF Trapani Salt Reserve and Marsala Stagnone. It is an oasis frequented by herons, egrets, pink flamingos and other birds typical of wetlands.

Trapani sea salt is born from the simple evaporation of sea water, thanks to the many winds that blow in this area off the Sicilian coast. And it is the wind, along with other natural elements such as sea water and the sun, that creates the so-called 'white gold'.

The salt flats are strikingly beautiful. They are made of water, windmills and white pyramids of salt. The colors of the salt are constantly changing, depending on the different stages of maturation: from blue to green, from pink to deep orange (after curing), and the dazzling white, shortly before harvest, which makes the flats look like ice fields on which to skate, or fields of fresh snow.

This salt has undisputed properties. It contains more potassium, more magnesium and a minor amount of sodium chloride. It also has an intense flavor, so you only need a small amount, compared to other types of salt.

Sea salt is obtained by the evaporation of sea water, which is introduced to the salt flats through an Archimedes coil (also known as a spiral). The water enters the first tank, then passes from one to another with a flow that is controlled by the skilled hands of man. The transition from one tank to another (the number of tanks varies with the abstention of saline), and the effect of evaporation due to sun and wind, determines an increase in salt concentration. In the servant tank, finally, the water becomes saturated and ready to be immersed in the salt pans, to deposit the sea salt. The cycle lasts from June to September. Weather permitting, the first crop is made after 50 days from the start of cultivation (in September), the second after 30 days. It is harvested by hand by workers with a shovel and wheelbarrow, and they make heaps of salt in 'Arioni' spaces in front of the salt pans.

Trapani sea salt is harvested by hand from the salari and does not undergo refining processes or washes that alter the properties. A humble product, Trapani sea salt contributes to the flavor of specialty Sicilian and Italian foods.

During your next trip to Sicily to discover its artistic and culinary heritage, be sure to visit this piece of Italian history where the salt pans date back to the year 500.

## AUTHOR'S NOTE

Butter:
If not specified, it is unsalted.

Cake tin measurements:
For cakes: 22 cm (8½ in) round tin (deep)
For pound-loaf cakes: 25 cm (10 in) (deep) loaf tin
For small cakes: 12-hole muffin tin or 12 cm (4½ in) round tin

Cheeses:
Italy produces more than 400 kinds of cheese. In this book, due to easy availability and knowledge, I preferred to use the best known abroad (Parmigiano, Fontina, Taleggio, Robiola, Gorgonzola...). If you have the chance to try other Italian specialty cheeses in your trusted stores, do not hesitate to add them into the recipes. If, however, you have difficulty in finding a cheese mentioned in the recipe or prefer to replace it with a cheese from your area, choose quality products with similar characteristics to the cheese indicated, so the taste does not differ too much from the one suggested. There are also excellent vegan cheeses, which I often use, that you can use to switch or replace the traditional one.

Eggs:
All used in these recipes are organic free range eggs at room temperature.

Flours:
All recipes that call for flour are tested with the whole flours indicated in the recipes. If you use refined white flours the amount of liquid ingredients change, as does the final result.

Fruit and vegetables:
All fruit and vegetables used in these recipes are organic. Remove the peel of fruit and skin of vegetables if they are not.

Organic or natural baking powder:
This means no dry chemical baking powder and it must be aluminum free. It is

available in the best supermarkets and organic food stores.

Oven:
The cooking times indicated may vary according to the type of oven (gas or electric).
I use a gas oven.

Unit of measure:
All measurements throughout this book are in grams (with the equivalent in
ounces). Measuring in ounces can be subject to changes in various English-
speaking countries, while gram is scientifically the most correct and accurate and
the most used around the world. A digital grams–ounces scale is the best purchase
that you can make to get the correct weight in grams.

'To taste':
Italian women, rather than cooking with scales and measuring cups, cook 'by eye'
(all'occhio), a term that, in Italy, you often hear, like 'to taste' (quanto basta). For
cooking 'by eye' you must have experience or, more simply, you have to adapt the
recipe, from time to time, according to the ingredients. For this reason, also in this
book, you will find, sometimes, the term to taste and not the equivalent in grams.
What maybe good for one home cook, might not be good for another.

AUTUMN

# BAKED PUMPKIN WITH MARINATED HERBS AND GORGONZOLA

*Zucca al forno con erbe marinate e Gorgonzola*

Not just a vegetable that welcomes you to the autumn table with its beautiful color, pumpkin also has a special charm which makes it perfect as an ornament in the kitchen.

When it is time, I choose those smaller in size (easier to use in home cooking) from the garden of close friends with whom, from time to time, we exchange vegetables with. This very easy recipe is great for a rustic lunch in the countryside. The cheese in this dish is a pillar of Italian tradition, from the north of the country: Gorgonzola. It is perfect to give the dish a refined and special taste. Of course, you can opt for other soft or semi-soft cheeses, preferring those intensely flavored but not too intrusive.

## Ingredients

1 small pumpkin
Extra virgin olive oil, to taste
2 sprigs of rosemary
Sea salt and black pepper, to taste
75 g (3 oz) Gorgonzola cheese

**Serves 2–4**

## Method

1. Wash the pumpkin under running water and rub thoroughly with a brush to remove any remaining dirt.
2. Cut it in half, remove the seeds and filaments inside with a spoon, then cut into cubes.
3. Transfer the pumpkin cubes to an oven tray, lined with baking paper. Season with extra virgin olive oil, rosemary, sea salt and black pepper.
4. Cook in the oven at 180°C (350°F/gas 4) for about 35 minutes (or until the pumpkin is tender).
5. When cooked, add the cheese, cut into cubes and serve.

# BROCCOLI SALAD
*Insalata di broccoli*

This is not just a salad or a side dish, but also a single dish, rich in vitamins, fiber and protein. This dish, simple but effective, has the characteristics that every salad should have: flavors, colors and textures. Broccoli, fresh from the garden, cooked al dente, crunchy toasted almonds and soft feta. You can also replace the feta cheese with rice or with tofu, taking care, in these cases, to add a pinch of salt.

## Ingredients

400 g (14 oz) broccoli
6 tbsp extra virgin olive oil
1 clove garlic
Crushed chili, to taste
50 g (2 oz) sliced white almonds
200 g (7 oz) Feta cheese, cubed
4 tbsp extra virgin olive oil
1 tbsp balsamic vinegar

**Serves 4**

## Method

1. Clean the broccoli and boil the peaks in salted water for 10 minutes.
2. Drain the broccoli and toss in a pan with 6 tablespoons oil, garlic and chili.
3. Cook for 5 minutes, adding 2 tablespoons of water to prevent drying.
4. Toast the almonds in a clean, dry pan for 3-4 minutes.
5. Pour the broccoli into a salad bowl, add the feta cheese and toasted almonds. Dress with 4 tablespoons extra virgin olive oil and 1 tablespoon balsamic vinegar.

# BROCCOLI CREAM WITH ONION
*Crema di broccoli con cipolla*

A classic autumn comfort food that I love preparing with harvested vegetables from my garden. If you don't believe this makes a difference, I recommend you give it a try. Vegetables grown without any pesticides have a mild taste and a delicate texture completely different to those sold in supermarkets. That is why even a simple cream like this is just great with the only addition being a high quality olive oil.

## Ingredients

300 g (11 oz) broccoli
2 onions (1 if large)
2 potatoes
400 ml (14 fl oz) water
Sea salt, to taste
Extra virgin olive oil, to taste
White pepper, to taste (optional)
2 slices rustic bread

**Serves 2**

## Method

1. Clean the broccoli, removing the hardest parts, and cut into small pieces.
2. Peel the onion and cut into chunks.
3. Peel the potatoes and then cook all the vegetables in a large pot of salted water for about 30 minutes.
4. When cooked, leave to cool and blend until the consistency is more or less creamy, according to taste. Put on the heat again for about 5 minutes.
5. Season with a little olive oil and, if desired, white pepper.
6. Serve immediately with rustic bread.

# BRUSCHETTA WITH GREEN TOFU SAUCE
*Bruschetta con salsa di tofu*

This seasoned bread, a typical Italian tradition, offers a wide possibility for simple and scrumptious ideas. This recipe, despite the presence of a non-Mediterranean ingredient, retains all the Italian flavors thanks to fresh oregano and capers, two key products of the Sicilian culinary tradition. A good olive oil (from Sicily or the Puglia region) is the necessary touch to give even more personality to this delicious, creamy sauce.

## Ingredients

100 g (3½ oz) natural tofu
1 tbsp extra virgin olive oil
Juice of one lemon
Pinch of sea salt and
  black pepper
1 heaped tbsp desalted
  capers
A handful of fresh
  oregano
A handful of mint
4 slices rustic toasted
  bread

**Serves 2–4**

## Method

1. In a mixer, crumble the tofu and add all the remaining ingredients apart from the bread.
2. Process until creamy (more or less creamy according to your taste. If necessary, for a more fluid cream, add a little water).
3. Transfer the sauce into a bowl and let stand in refrigerator for about 30 minutes.
4. Spread the sauce over the slices of toasted bread and serve immediately.

# CACIO E PEPE PASTA

*Pasta Cacio e Pepe*

Like other pasta dishes, typical of Italian culinary tradition, Cacio e Pepe (cheese and pepper) shows how a quality product wins over quantity. Only three simple but top-notch ingredients, give rise to a special and unique dish.

This is classic Italian culinary excellence, born from the tradition of shepherds who, on their long journeys, brought with them dry pasta, pecorino cheese and pepper.

The key to this recipe comes from the quality of the ingredients. Excellent Italian durum wheat pasta and aged pecorino PDO make the difference, allowing, once mixed together, and with the right amount of cooking water, the formation of the 'cream' that is characteristic of the recipe.

Long pasta (bucatini spaghetti) is preferable for this type of sauce.

## Ingredients

320 g (11¾ oz) bucatini pasta
100 g (3 ½ oz) high quality PDO pecorino cheese, grated
White pepper, to taste

**Serves 4**

## Method

1. Cook the pasta until al dente in boiling salted water. Drain the pasta and pour it into a pot.
2. Add 4 tablespoons of the cooking water and the pecorino cheese.
3. Mix well over a low heat for 2-3 minutes.
4. Add white pepper to taste and serve.

# CARROTS AND DRIED FRUIT SALAD

*Insalata di carote e frutta secca*

There is something special in salads. I think they are the symbol of the freedom to create, especially for home cooks. We are free to make something very simple and quick with our own hands and the vegetables available in the kitchen. Just like this autumn-winter salad, which has the color of the sun, given by carrots, and the warm shades of dried fruits.

The quality and freshness of the ingredients is critical to create a dish rich in flavor and with a crunchy texture. Perfect as appetizer, side dish or as a nutritious snack.

## Ingredients

6 carrots
Juice of 1 lemon
A handful of almonds
A handful of hazelnuts
A handful of raisins
Extra virgin olive oil, to taste
Sea salt and black pepper, to taste

**Serves 2**

## Method

1. Peel the carrots, cut them into circles and place in a bowl.
2. Add the lemon juice.
3. Coarsely chop the almonds and hazelnuts and then add to the bowl.
4. Carefully wash the raisins and add to the salad. Season with a generous dose of extra virgin olive oil, and add salt and pepper to taste.
5. Let stand for 10 minutes before serving so that the flavors blend together.

# CHEESE TRUFFLES
*Tártufi di formaggio*

Soft goat's cheese (caprino cheese) is one of the Italian specialty cheeses. A good goat's milk cheese has a strong but not invasive flavor. As one of the classic Italian appetizers it is served as small truffles covered with chopped dried fruit (pistachios, almonds, hazelnuts).

Although this recipe goes well throughout the year, I love to prepare it in the autumn when Sicilian pistachios are available with all their unique taste.

You can find pistachio flour in the supermarkets but, if you want a unique, fresh taste, my suggestion is to buy whole pistachios and blend them at the time of preparing the recipe.

## Ingredients

200 g (7 oz) Italian caprino soft cheese (soft goat's cheese), or other soft cheese
100 g (3½ oz) high quality pistachio flour, or chopped pistachios

**Serves 4**

## Method

1. Take small portions of cheese and form into balls.
2. Dip the mini cheese balls in the chopped pistachios.
3. Store in refrigerator until ready to serve.

# SAVORY CAKE WITH CHEESE AND PEAR

*Tòrta salata di formaggio e pere*

On autumn Sundays spent in the countryside with friends, savory cakes are one of those pleasant habits that keep us women occupied in the kitchen while the men are busy with their chatter.

This recipe is great for a brunch or a sea salty snack. The quality of the cheese is essential not only for taste but also for texture. Grana cheese has a very delicate flavor and is ideal for recipes like this.

## Ingredients

250 g (9 oz) wholemeal Farro flour

2 tbsp organic baking powder

Black pepper, to taste

200 g (7 oz) grated Grana cheese

2 large eggs

Pinch of sea salt

75 ml (3 fl oz) milk, at room temperature

5 tbsp extra virgin olive oil

1 pear (2 if small)

A sprig of fresh (or dried) oregano

**Serves 8–10**

## Method

1. Preheat the oven to 180° C (350° F/gas 4).
2. Sift the flour and baking powder. Add the pepper, grated cheese, eggs, sea salt and mix.
3. Pour in the room temperature milk and olive oil and mix again.
4. Peel the pear, cut it into cubes and mix it into the dough with the oregano.
5. Pour the mixture into a mold, lined with parchment paper (or oiled and floured).
6. Bake for 35 minutes.

# GRAPE SALAD

*Insalata di uva*

---

When I was a child, the end of summer and early autumn was one of the best times of the year because while the adults were busy with the harvest we children were playing carefree in the countryside tasting the juicy berries of generous vines.

During the breaks in the harvest, young and old would sit around a large table and grapes were served in so many ways. Among these, I remember a fresh salad made with the ingredients from my mother and other women participating in what was a veritable feast. The grape quality is the key to making this simple recipe very special.

## Ingredients

Extra virgin olive oil, to taste

Juice of 1 lemon

Sea salt, to taste

Black pepper, to taste

150 g (5 oz) romaine (or other green) lettuce

200 g (7 oz) red grapes

2 pears

50 g (2 oz) Parmigiano cheese

**Serves 4**

## Method

1. Prepare an emulsion with the oil, lemon, salt and pepper.
2. Beat the dressing with a fork to combine.
3. Wash the lettuce, grapes and pears (remove the skin from the pears only if they are not organic).
4. Coarsely chop lettuce, slice the grapes in half and remove the seeds, dice the pear (keeping the skin, if organic) and flake the Parmigiano.
5. Arrange the salad in a bowl or on a large plate. Pour over the emulsion and serve.

# MIXED SALAD
*Insalata mista*

---

This classic salad is perfect as an appetizer, side dish or a light dinner, accompanied, for example, with veggie burgers, boiled eggs and good rustic bread toasted and cut into cubes.

The artichoke hearts in oil and olives are two of the ingredients that give that extra touch to even the most simple salad.

## Ingredients

8 romaine salad leaves
8 radicchio leaves
Half a head of curly
  lettuce
2 tbsp toasted almonds
10 pitted olives (black
  and/or green)
8 artichoke hearts in oil
1 tbsp balsamic vinegar
3 tbsp extra virgin olive
  oil
Oregano, to taste
Sea salt and black
  pepper, to taste
Half a red chili, diced

**Serves 4**

## Method

1. Wash all salads, dry and chop. Coarsely chop the almonds, olives and artichokes.
2. Mix all ingredients in a bowl. Season with balsamic vinegar, extra virgin olive oil, oregano, salt, pepper and half a chili.

# PASTA WITH RADICCHIO AND STRACCHINO

*Pasta con radicchio e stracchino*

For us Italians pasta is the comfort food par excellence, the first course that we learn to cook, the first dish we choose for a sudden dinner (or lunch) with friends.

In Italy, every town has 'its' pasta recipe, and even pasta with tomato sauce, while containing the same ingredients, can have so many different methods of cooking.

Radicchio lettuce and Stracchino cheese are two typical ingredients of northern Italian cuisine and the heroes of this creamy, greedy pasta sauce. Stracchino is a soft cheese produced only with whole milk. Its delicate flavor goes perfectly with the bitter taste of radicchio.

## Ingredients

Extra virgin olive oil, to taste
1 red onion, finely chopped
Half ahead of radicchio
150 g (5 oz) Stracchino cheese (or other soft cheese)
3 tbsp organic milk
160 g (5 oz) short pasta
Sea salt and black pepper to taste

**Serves 2**

## Method

1. In a frypan heat the oil. Add the finely chopped onion and fry.
2. Wash the radicchio, finely chop, put into the pan and cook until tender.
3. In a separate saucepan, melt the Stracchino cheese with the milk. Add the creamy cheese to the radicchio and set aside.
4. Cook the pasta until al dente in boiling salted water. Drain the pasta, leaving a little of the cooking water.
5. Toss the pasta with the sauce and serve immediately.

# PIZZA MARGHERITA
*Pizza Margherita*

Pizza is one of the dishes most representative of Italy. Like many other traditional Italian culinary creations, it also sinks its history between myth and reality. The setting of this story is south Italy, where the basics of Italian cuisine and the magic city of Naples have produced many iconic Italian dishes.

It was the summer of 1889, when King Umberto I and Queen Margherita of Savoy resided in the palace of Capodimonte, near Naples. The queen had already heard of the famous Neapolitan pizza and, wanting to taste it, she called the most renowned pizza maker of the time, Don Raffaele. He, together with his wife, prepared three different types of pizza that had the colors of the Italian flag: one with cheese and basil; one with garlic, oil and tomato and another with tomato, mozzarella and basil. The queen liked the latter so much that Don Raffaele gave her name to the pizza, although this type of pizza already existed and was known and appreciated throughout the city.

It is a simple dish and, because of this, difficult to achieve the best. What makes the Margherita pizza is the perfect blend of high quality flour and the characteristics of the water in the area. In Italy, you can eat a great pizza from north to south but the world capital of pizza is Naples.

At home it is not always easy to make a good pizza (often, it depends on the oven, which, of course, can't compete with a stone woodfire oven). In any case, even homemade pizza is one of those pleasures to be enjoyed, using simple but first choice ingredients (pizza, like pasta, will not make you fat if made with a few, genuine ingredients).

Water, unrefined ancient Farro flour, extra virgin olive oil, tomatoes and mozzarella cheese are the main ingredients of my basic recipe.

## Ingredients

500 g (17 oz) white Farro
  (or Kamut) flour
Sea salt, to taste
12 g (¼ oz) organic
  instant dry yeast
500 ml (17 fl oz) warm
  water
1 clove garlic
4 tbsp extra virgin olive
  oil
500 ml (17 fl oz) tomato
  pulp
1 sprig basil
150 g (5 oz) mozzarella
Dry oregano, to taste

**Serves 2–4**

## Method

1.  Mix together the Farro or Kamut flour, salt, instant
    dry yeast and add warm water little by little until
    you get a soft dough,.
2.  Let the mixture rise for 20 minutes (recommended
    time, only if you use instant yeast).
3.  Brown the garlic in a little extra virgin olive oil.
    Remove it and cook the tomato pulp until the sauce
    is thick (around 15 minutes).
4.  When the tomato is cooked, add more extra virgin
    olive oil to taste and the basil.
5.  Roll out the dough onto an oiled baking tray. Pour
    over the tomato sauce. Slice the mozzarella cheese
    and place over the tomato.
6.  Season with plenty more extra virgin olive oil and
    oregano.
7.  Bake at 180°C (350°F/gas 4) for 30 minutes.

# MASHED POTATOES IN PUFF PASTRY PIE

*Purea di patate in pasta sfoglia*

This dish is perfect for picnics, a brunch or an easy dinner. You can prepare it the day before and warm or cold, it expresses all its flavors after resting for 24 hours.

I usually prepare it with a typical Sicilian cheese that gives a particular creaminess. Of course, feel free to substitute with another cheese of your choice, provided it is of high quality.

## Ingredients

6 large potatoes
2 leeks
60 g (2 oz) butter
A handful capers
Sea salt, to taste
Black pepper, to taste
1 sheet puff pastry
100 g (3½ oz) Sicilian
  cheese with pepper, or
  Taleggio cheese, diced

**Serves 4–6**

## Method

1. Peel the potatoes and wash, then cut and wash the leeks and cook together. Once soft, drain them and stir through the butter.
2. Add the capers, salt, freshly ground black pepper and mash.
3. Roll out the pastry on a baking sheet, greased or covered with baking paper.
4. Cover with the mashed potatoes, and add the cheese.
5. Bake, in a preheated oven, for 20 minutes at 180°C (350°F/gas 4).

# PIZZA WITH GORGONZOLA CHEESE AND PISTACHIO

*Pizza con Gorgonzola e pistacchio*

Among the many recipes that you can create with a good pizza dough, this is one of the most delicious. Ideal in the cold months, this freshly baked pizza with Gorgonzola reveals all the flavor of one of the most appreciated and versatile Italian cheeses.

Pistachio is the added twist that gives a particular scent and unique flavor to this pizza, perfect when served freshly baked.

## Ingredients

500 g (17 oz) white Kamut flour
Sea salt, to taste
12 g (¼ oz) organic instant dry yeast
500 ml (17 fl oz) water
250 g (9 oz) soft sweet Gorgonzola cheese (Gorgonzola dolce)
Extra virgin olive oil, to taste
150 g (5 oz) chopped pistachios

**Serves 2–4**

## Method

1. Mix together the flour, salt and instant dry yeast, adding the water little by little, until you get a soft dough.
2. Let the mixture rise for 20 minutes (recommended time, only if you use instant yeast).
3. Roll out the dough on an oiled baking tray. Cut the Gorgonzola into cubes and sprinkle over. Add the extra virgin olive oil to taste and chopped pistachios.
4. Bake at 180°C (350°F/gas 4) for 30 minutes.
5. Serve hot.

# POLENTA AND CHEESES

*Polenta e formaggi*

Polenta was the poor food of the farmers of northern Italy. For them, meat was a luxury and polenta was often enriched with different seasonings which gave the possibility to vary the meal each day, despite always using the same basic ingredient.

Today, polenta is still eaten mainly in the north of the country but, of course, the recipes are rich in all those quality Italian products that make it a dish of excellence.

This is one of the best-known and simplest recipes, perfect eaten hot or cold.

Delicious served in individual serving cocottes, it is ideal not only as an appetizer or snack but also as a main dish for brunch.

## Ingredients

300 g (11 oz) precooked polenta

150 g (5 oz) spinach

500 ml (17fl oz) water

Sea salt, to taste

Extra virgin olive oil, to taste

12 cubes of Fontina cheese

**Serves 6**

## Method

1. Cook the polenta in boiling salted water for 10 minutes or according to the instructions on the pack.
2. Wash the spinach and cook in a pan, for about 10 minutes, adding a glass of water. Halfway through cooking, add a pinch of salt and oil.
3. Grease 6 medium molds, fill with some of the polenta, add 1 or 2 cubes of Fontina cheese and cover with a spoonful of spinach.
4. Bake at 180°C (350°F/gas 4) for 15 minutes.

# POTATO CAKE
*Torta di patate*

This is one of those comfort foods that tastes like home.

   A traditional classic Italian dish that can be seasoned in various ways, according to your taste and the season. This version has all the creaminess of one of the most well-known Italian soft cheeses, Crescenza. Ideal served hot or cold, this is a traditional dish for an informal brunch or picnic.

## Ingredients

500 g (17 oz) potatoes
Sea salt and black
   pepper, to taste
Extra virgin olive oil, to
   taste
4 tbsp breadcrumbs
100 g (3 ½ oz) Crescenza
   soft cheese
50 g (2 oz) grated
   Parmigiano Reggiano

**Serves 6–8**

## Method

1. Wash the potatoes and steam cook them for about 20 minutes (cut the potatoes into similar sizes for uniform cooking). Drain the potatoes, mash and season with salt and pepper. Add the extra virgin olive oil and mix.
2. Lightly oil a baking dish, sprinkle 2 tbsp of breadcrumbs and pour in the mixture.
3. On top, add the Crescenza cheese broken into pieces, grated Parmigiano and the last tablespoons of breadcrumbs. Bake at 180° C (350°F/gas 4) for 25 minutes.

# PUMPKIN SOUP
*Zuppa di zucca*

A classic autumn soup, this recipe is a comfort food that warms and nourishes with taste. I love to make it in the simplest way and with the addition of another orange vegetable – carrots.

Rich in beta-carotene and vitamins, this soup is ideal accompanied with slices of freshly baked rustic bread.

## Ingredients

400 g (14 oz) pumpkin
3 carrots
1 onion
Sea salt, to taste
Black pepper, to taste
Parmigiano cheese, to taste
Extra virgin olive oil, to taste

**Serves 4**

## Method

1. Chop and peel the pumpkin, peel the carrots and cut the onion into large pieces.
2. Season with salt and steam the vegetables for 20 minutes.
3. Puree with a hand blender until smooth and creamy.
4. Add pepper, Parmigiano and extra virgin olive oil to taste and serve warm.

# RADICCHIO AND APPLE SLAW WITH MODICA SEA SALT CHOCOLATE

*Insalata di radicchio e mele con cioccolato di Modica al sale*

The evolution of Italian home cooking does not erase traditions but renews and, in some cases, improves it. Attention to healthier cooking that emphasizes fruits and vegetables can give life to creations that were once unusual but that now embrace the best Italian products.

Red apples from the Trentino region (northern Italy) join the radicchio from Treviso and Sicilian Modica chocolate in a marriage of flavors that celebrate the north and south of the country with a salad of refined taste.

## Ingredients

2 red apples
Half a head of radicchio
Extra virgin olive oil, to taste
Toasted sesame seeds
White pepper, to taste
50 g (2 oz) grated Modica chocolate, sea salt flavor

**Serves 2**

## Method

1. Wash and dry the apples, remove the core and cut into strips.
2. Wash and dry the radicchio leaves and cut into strips.
3. In a bowl, mix the oil with toasted sesame seeds and pepper. Add the fruit and vegetable.
4. Coarsely chop or grate the chocolate, according to your taste and sprinkle over the salad.

# RIGATONI WITH CAULIFLOWER AND PECORINO

*Rigatoni con cavolfiore e Pecorino*

I've learnt to appreciate this dish over the years. Among the many specialties prepared by my mother, this is still one of her best. It was one of her 'smart' ways to get her daughters to eat vegetables. Today, it is one of the inevitable dishes on my autumn table. The satisfaction and taste are even greater with the small and tasty cauliflower from our family garden. Olives and cheese are the key to this nutritious pasta dish.

## Ingredients

1 medium cauliflower

Extra virgin olive oil, to taste

Sea salt, to taste

50 g (2 oz) black pitted olives

50 ml (2 fl oz) sparkling wine

320 g (11 ½) rigatoni (or other short pasta)

Grated pecorino, to taste

**Serves 4**

## Method

1. Peel and cut the cauliflower and steam cook.
2. Once cooked, pour the cauliflower into a saucepan, with olive oil, sea salt, olives and the sparkling wine. Saute for 5 minutes.
3. Cook the pasta until al dente, in boiling salted water.
4. Pour the cauliflower sauce over the pasta, season with Pecorino and serve immediately.

# SAVORY COOKIES WITH ROBIOLA CHEESE

*Biscottini salati con Robiola*

Particularly suitable as a starter, for a drink or snack, these cookies are one of my most pleasant preparations.

The rustic flavor of the cookies made with honey joins the creaminess of the Robiola cheese for a winning combination.

## Ingredients

100 g (3½ oz) brown rice flour, sifted

200 g (7 oz) wholewheat flour, sifted

50 g (2 oz) puffed brown rice

75 ml (3 fl oz) mild extra virgin olive oil

1 large beaten egg

50 g (2 oz) raw honey

Sea salt and black pepper to taste

200 g (7 oz) Robiola cheese

1 tbsp white wine

1 tbsp olive oil

**Makes about 25 cookies**

## Method

1. Mix the flours with the puffed brown rice, oil, egg, honey and a pinch of salt and pepper. Knead until a smooth ball.
2. Mix the soft cheese with 1 tablespoon of wine and 1 tablespoon olive oil. Leave to rest in the refrigerator.
3. Roll out the dough with a rolling pin on a floured surface and cut out lots of little cookie disks. Place them on a baking sheet and bake at 180°C (350°F/ gas 4) for 15 minutes.
4. Remove the cookies from the oven and let cool.
5. Spread with the Robiola cream on the flat side of the cookies, then put the remaining cookies on top and enjoy.

# SICILIAN SPICY FARFALLE

*Farfalle speziate alla siciliana*

Dry spices are the hero of Sicilian cuisine. Oregano, garlic, crushed red chilis and sun-dried tomatoes are sold in transparent individual bags in Italian specialty stores (in some cases, even in the best supermarkets) and they are ready to flavor delicious pasta dishes or salads. The result is a dish with a very distinct taste that reminds you of the taste of southern Italian home cooking.

## Ingredients

50 g (2 oz) dried oregano
50 g (2 oz) dried chili flakes
50 g (2 oz) dried garlic flakes
50 g (2 oz) chopped sun-dried tomatoes
Sea salt, to taste
200 g (7 oz) wholewheat Farfalle pasta
Extra virgin olive oil, to taste

**Serves 2**

## Method

1. In a bowl, mix together all the aromas with a pinch of salt and set aside.
2. Cook the pasta until al dente, in boiling salted water.
3. Once cooked, drain the pasta, leaving a little of the cooking water in the pan. Season with the spicy aromas, add extra virgin olive oil and serve.

# SMALL CAKES WITH OREGANO, PISTACHIO AND PECORINO

*Tortine con origano, pistacchio e pecorino*

These gluten-free small cakes are one of my favorite afternoon snacks. Accompanied with a soft cheese and/or whole raw vegetables they are a delicious alternative to traditional sweet cake breaks.

The flavor of Pecorino matches perfectly with the delicate crispness of pistachio. The fresh oregano, which in early autumn still smells beautiful, finishes a winning combination of ingredients in this recipe.

## Ingredients

1 large egg
75 ml (3 fl oz) extra virgin olive oil
100 ml (3½ fl oz) organic milk
100 g (3½ oz) Pecorino cheese
Pinch of sea salt
300 g (11 oz) brown rice flour, sifted
15 g (½ oz) organic baking powder
Fresh oregano, to taste
Pistachio, to garnish

**Serves 10–12**

## Method

1. Preheat oven to 180°C (350°F/gas 4).
2. Beat the egg with the oil and milk. Add the Pecorino, salt, sifted flour, baking powder and fresh oregano and mix the ingredients together.
3. Pour the batter into muffin molds, sprinkle the surface with pistachios.
4. Bake for 15 minutes.

# AMARETTI CHOCOLATE CUPS

*Crema di cioccolato fondente con amaretti*

These cups are a simple but refined dessert. The unique taste and the crunchy texture of Italian Amaretti goes perfectly with dark chocolate ganache and fresh cream.

You can make this recipe in a few minutes and serve immediately as the cream fondant, especially if stored in a refrigerator, tends to solidify.

## Ingredients

20 amaretti cookies (biscuits)
200 g (7 oz) dark 70% chocolate
50 g (2 oz) dark 60% chocolate
50 g (2 oz) butter
125 ml (4 fl oz) fresh whipping cream

**Serves 2**

## Method

1. Crumble 10 amaretti in each cup and set aside.
2. Melt the chocolate with the butter. Once it has cooled, pour the cream-ganache over the amaretti.
3. Whip the cream and fill the glass with a generous dose.
4. Decorate with the remaining amaretti, crushed, and serve immediately.

# CREAMY PEARS, BANANA AND CINNAMON SMOOTHIE

*Smoothie cremoso di pere, banane e cannella*

I love this creamy dessert smoothie, with its velvety texture and fulfilling flavor. The banana is one of the main ingredients of this recipe because its texture makes it ideal to give the right consistency.

Pears, sweet and juicy, are among the most welcome autumn fruits and mean these smoothie cups are ideal to serve for breakfast or for an afternoon break.

## Ingredients

3 ripe pears
1 banana
1 tbsp raw honey
100 g (3½ oz) high quality fresh ricotta
50 ml (2 fl oz) organic milk
Ground cinnamon, to taste

**Serves 2**

## Method

1. Wash the pears (and peel them if not organic).
2. Cut the banana and caramelize in a hot pan with the honey. Allow to cool and then put in a blender.
3. Add the ricotta and milk and whisk at maximum power.
4. Pour into glasses and decorate with ground cinnamon.
5. Store in the refrigerator until just before serving.

# TIRAMISU CUPS

*Coppe tiramisu*

The creation of tiramisu is disputed between Tuscany, Piedmont and Veneto. According to a Tuscan legend, tiramisu was born in the 17th century in Siena by some confectioners who wanted to celebrate the arrival and the grandeur of the Grand Duke of Tuscany, Cosimo de Medici. The tiramisu was called *Zuppa del Duca* ('Duke's soup') in honor of Cosimo de Medici. Again according to this legend, tiramisu became the favorite dessert of the nobles for its aphrodisiac power, which is why this name, in a metaphorical sense, can be translated into the phrase 'Make me feel good'.

Another legend holds that the cake was invented by a pastry chef from Turin, in Piedmont, to honor Count Camillo Benso di Cavour, active in the unification of Italy.

Both stories are, in turn, denied by another belief, that the tiramisu comes from the tradition of the city of Treviso, in Veneto. In this region of northern Italy, at one time, people gave an energetic sweet prepared with beaten egg and sugar to children and the elderly, called, in the local dialect, *El sbatudin*. An imaginative chef-confectioner, Loli Linguanotto added mascarpone, savoiardi cookies (ladyfingers), cocoa and bitter coffee.

## Ingredients

10 savoiardi cookies (lady fingers)
50 ml (2 fl oz) espresso coffee
150 ml (5 fl oz) fresh cream
1 tbsp raw sugar (optional)
Cocoa powder to taste

**Serves 2**

## Method

1. Soak the savoiardi cookies in the coffee and place a first layer in the bottom of the glass.
2. Whip the cream, adding, if you like, a tablespoon of light brown sugar and cover the cookies.
3. Arrange another layer of savoiardi and cream, finishing with a third layer if the size of the cup allows.
4. Decorate with cocoa powder.

# PEAR AND CHOCOLATE CAKE
*Torta di pere*

Although my undisputed love for chocolate cakes lasts all year, I admit that autumn is the best time to welcome the long season of soft and fluffy cakes.

The lightness of the brown rice flour (gluten-free) fits perfectly with the rest of the ingredients. Rum enhances the flavor of the raw chocolate. Pears break the bitterness of the chocolate with their sweetness and make this delicious cake pleasantly moist.

## Ingredients

2 large eggs
75 g (3 oz) raw honey
100 ml (3 ½ fl oz) plain yogurt
75 ml (3 fl oz) mild extra virgin olive oil
100 ml (3 ½ fl oz) melted dark 70% chocolate
50 g (2 oz) melted dark 80% chocolate
1 tbsp rum
200 g (7 oz) brown rice flour, sifted
15 g (½ oz) organic baking powder
2 pears

**Serves 8–10**

## Method

1. Preheat the oven to 180°C (350°F/gas 4).
2. Whip the eggs with the honey. Add the yogurt, olive oil, and melted and cooled chocolate. Add the rum.
3. Mix the flour with the baking powder and add it to the batter, stirring from the bottom upwards.
4. Pour into a mold, oiled and floured (or lined with parchment paper).
5. Wash, core and cut the pears in half and arrange over the top of the cake.
6. Bake for 35–40 minutes.

# SOFT MODICA CHOCOLATE AND PISTACHIO CAKE

*Torta morbida al cioccolato di Modica con pistacchio*

Ideal as an energy giving breakfast, this ciambella (doughnut) celebrates some of the most noble Sicilian products: Modica chocolate, Marsala (a dessert wine that is named after the Sicilian town where it is made) and pistachios. Apparently an ordinary chocolate cake but one that, once tasted, reveals all the unique delicacy of the special ingredients. The pureed raisins are a great alternative to sugar.

## Ingredients

200 g (7 oz) Modica dark bitter chocolate
2 tbsp Marsala dessert wine
3 large eggs, separated
Pinch of sea salt
150 g (5 oz) pureed raisins (previously washed and left to soak in warm water for 15 minutes and then pureed in a blender at full power)
1 tbsp honey
75 ml (3 fl oz) mild extra virgin olive oil
300 g (11 oz) pistachio flour
150 g (5 oz) wholewheat flour, sifted
1 tsp organic baking powder
Pistachios, to taste, chopped

## Method

1. Preheat the oven to 180°C (350°F/gas 4).
2. Melt the chocolate and, off the heat, add the 2 tablespoons of Marsala. Allow to cool.
3. Whip the egg whites with a pinch of salt and set aside.
4. Beat the egg yolks with the pureed raisins and honey. Add the oil, the pistachio flour, wholewheat flour and baking powder.
5. Combine with the egg whites and mix from the bottom up. Add the melted chocolate and stir it in quickly.
6. Oil and flour a ciambella-doughnut cake tin and pour in the mixture. Sprinkle the surface with a generous dose of pistachios. Bake for 35–40 minutes.

**Serves 8–10**

# RICOTTA AND ALMOND CAKE

*Torta di ricotta e mandorle*

The ricotta that I buy from my local farm is so exquisite it has become the hero of many recipes, both sweet and savory.

This cake remains soft for some days but be assured that, once ready, it will not last long as it is so tasty in its simplicity. It has a very delicate sweetness because of the raw honey that is the only sweetener. The cake is also suitable to be coated with a delicious homemade jam. I also love to serve this cake as dessert, covering it with a delicious honey glaze.

## Ingredients

300 g (9 oz) whole almonds
50 g (2 oz) white Farro flour, sifted
15 g (½ oz) organic baking powder
8 tbsp raw honey
3 large beaten eggs
250 g (9 oz) ricotta
2 tbsp extra virgin olive oil

**Serves 8–10**

## Method

1. Preheat the oven to 180°C (350°F/gas 4).
2. Finely chop the almonds. Add the flour, baking powder, 6 tablespoons honey, beaten eggs and ricotta cheese. Mix the ingredients until the dough is creamy.
3. Grease a cake mold with oil, and pour in the dough.
4. Bake for 45–50 minutes until golden.
5. In a saucepan, melt 2 tablespoons of honey over a medium heat. Pour the glaze over the cake and serve. If desired, you can also serve the cake, cut into cubes. In this case, cut the cake before adding the icing.

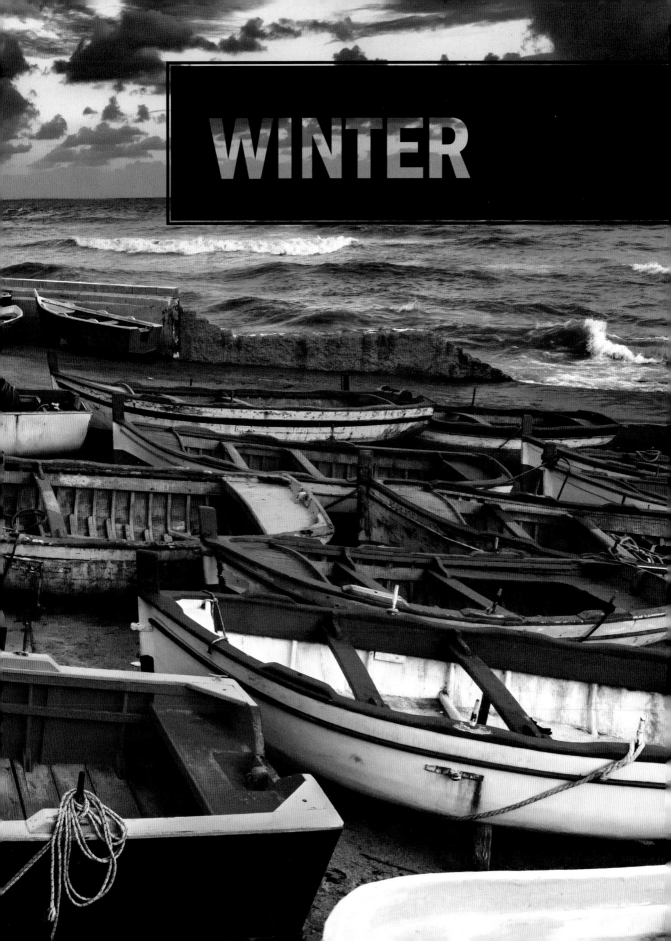

# WINTER

# APPLE AND ROCKET (ARAGULA) SALAD

*Insalata di mele e rucola*

Salads are one of the basics of the Italian diet all year round and not just in summer. And if you think they are unattractive, then you do not know the many variations that can be created with easy and inexpensive ingredients. This salad, for example, is not only suitable as an appetizer or side dish but it can also become a great afternoon snack, especially for students.

## Ingredients

2 organic red apples

A generous handful of rocket (arugula) and lettuce salad

2 fennel bulbs

A handful of walnuts

A handful of raisins

Extra virgin olive oil, to taste

Sea salt and black pepper, to taste

1 tbsp cider vinegar

**Serves 2**

## Method

1. Thoroughly clean the fruits and vegetables and dry well.
2. Cut the apple into slices along with the fennel.
3. In a bowl, place the salad leaves and add the apple and fennel.
4. Add a handful of nuts and raisins (the latter washed and dried) and drizzle with olive oil, salt and pepper to taste, and cider vinegar.

# APPLE SALAD WITH ROBIOLA CHEESE AND WALNUTS

*Insalata di mele con Robiola e noci*

This salad is a real concentration of vitamins and a tempting way to refresh the palate in a meal that includes several courses.

It is also a delicious and crunchy snack for the afternoon break. You can replace the walnuts with other dried fruit to your liking, while apples are the best combination with radicchio.

## Ingredients

1 apple
Juice of 1 lemon
50 g (2 oz) chopped
   walnuts
150 g (5 oz) Robiola
   cheese, diced
Pinch of sea salt
4 tbsp extra virgin olive
   oil

**Serves 4**

## Method

1. Wash the apple, remove the core and cut into cubes. Drizzle the apple with lemon juice to prevent it browning.
2. Drain the apples and mix with the nuts. Add the diced Robiola, pinch of salt, olive oil and mix.
3. Serve immediately.

# ARTICHOKE HEARTS WITH BREADCRUMBS

*Cuori di carciofo con briciole di pane tostato*

A recipe typical of the Sicilian tradition, a delicious side dish that also becomes a great appetizer to be served with a potato cake, cut into cubes or squares of crispy buns.

For the breadcrumbs, choose the crust of a good rustic crispy bread. This, along with a good oil, will make the difference.

## Ingredients

100 g (3½ oz)
  breadcrumbs
15 artichoke hearts
Sea salt, to taste
2 untreated lemons
Extra virgin olive oil, to
  taste
1 tbsp dried red chili
1 tbsp dried oregano

**Serves 5**

## Method

1. Saute the breadcrumbs in a pan for 5 minutes.
2. Clean the artichoke hearts, add a pinch of salt and cut two lemons into wedges.
3. Put everything into a baking dish and season with extra virgin olive oil, dried red chili, oregano and the breadcrumbs.
4. Put in the oven at 180°C (350°F/gas 4) and brown for 20 minutes.

# BAKED RADICCHIO WITH POTATOES AND GORGONZOLA

*Radicchio al forno con Gorgonzola*

---

Radicchio is a very valuable vegetable, the hero of many recipes in northern Italy. It is very versatile, ideal for appetizers, salads and side dishes. This recipe is a great side dish with many nutritional properties.

It is best to serve freshly baked to better enjoy the crispness of the radicchio leaves and the unmistakable flavor of the melted Gorgonzola.

## Ingredients

4 potatoes
Pinch of sea salt
4 heads of radicchio from
    Treviso
Black pepper, to taste
Juice of one lemon
Extra virgin olive oil, to
    taste
150 g (5 oz) Gorgonzola
    cheese, cubed

**Serves 4**

## Method

1. Preheat the oven to 180°C (350°F/Gas 4).
2. Peel the potatoes, finely cut into rounds (or according to your taste). Place on a baking sheet covered with parchment paper and cook for about 20 minutes (cooking time varies depending on the size of the potatoes).
3. Once cooked, season the potatoes with salt and set aside.
4. Cut the radicchio into wedges removing the toughest part of the root. Rinse well and drain, dry with a towel. Put it in an oiled baking pan and season with salt and pepper and the juice of a lemon.
5. Bake the radicchio at 180°C (350°F/gas 4) for 15 minutes.
6. Once you've baked the radicchio, add the potatoes and Gorgonzola pieces.

# BROCCOLI AND FONTINA SMALL CAKES

*Tortine di broccoli e Fontina*

---

Served as appetizers or delicious snacks, these savory small cakes are complete from a nutritional point of view, containing carbohydrate, protein and vitamins.

Perfect for a brunch, they are ideal with a mix of salads or crudités and a good glass of wine.

## Ingredients

100 g (3 ½ oz) broccoli

200 g (7 oz) wholewheat flour, sifted

15 g (½ oz) organic baking powder for savory cakes

Generous pinch of sea salt

75 g (3 oz) grated Parmigiano Reggiano cheese

100 g (3½ oz) Taleggio cheese, cut into cubes

White pepper, to taste

2 large eggs

125 ml (4 ½ fl oz) extra virgin olive oil

**Serves 10–12**

## Method

1. Cut the broccoli, removing the leaves and the hardest parts. Cook in salted water for 15 minutes, drain and set aside.
2. Preheat the oven to 180°C (350°F/gas 4).
3. Mix together the dry ingredients – the flour, baking powder, salt, Parmigiano and Taleggio cheese and white pepper.
4. Beat the eggs, and add oil, continuing until it emulsifies. Gradually, add the dry ingredients, stirring quickly. Then add the broccoli.
5. Place the dough in appropriate cake molds (12-hole muffin tin or a 12 cm (4½ in) round tin) and bake for 12–15 minutes.

# CASTELLANE PASTA WITH ALMOND PESTO

*Castellane con pesto di mandorle*

Pesto is strictly made with raw ingredients and its goodness comes from the flavors emanating from top quality products.

The best almonds from Sicily and the sage from my garden are among the ingredients in this tasteful and nutritious pesto, great for giving energy in cold weather.

## Ingredients

100 g (3½ oz) almonds
5 sage leaves
Extra virgin olive, to taste
50 g (2 oz) grated
   Parmigiano cheese, to
   taste
1 tbsp grated Pecorino
   cheese
Pinch of sea salt
320 g (11 ¼ oz)
   Castellane or other
   short pasta

**Serves 4**

## Method

1. Blend the almonds with the sage and olive oil. Add the Parmigiano, Pecorino, salt and a little more olive oil (if necessary, dilute with a little water).
2. Cook the pasta until al dente in boiling salted water.
3. Drain then stir through the almond pesto.
4. Serve immediately.

# BROCCOLI AU GRATIN
*Broccoli gratinati*

A classic Italian side dish that becomes delicious with quality ingredients. In this case, the difference is made by organic broccoli and the best Taleggio cheese. A northern Italian soft cheese with washed rind and an intense flavor, Taleggio is ideal in recipes such as this because it melts easily (you can replace it with Fontina cheese, or with other local soft cheese to your liking).

## Ingredients

500g (17 oz) broccoli
1 tbsp extra virgin olive oil
Sea salt, to taste
100 g (3½ oz) Taleggio cheese (or other soft cheese), cut into cubes
2 tbsp breadcrumbs

**Serves 2**

## Method

1. Clean the broccoli and detach the florets from the core. Steam the broccoli for 15 minutes (or boil for 8 minutes in salted water). Drain them, grease a baking dish with oil, place the cheese in the bottom, then gently place the broccoli over the top.
2. Add a drizzle of olive oil, a pinch of salt and sprinkle with breadcrumbs.
3. Bake for 15–20 minutes.
4. Serve immediately.

# CHICKPEA SOUP
*Zuppa di ceci*

The basis of the Mediterranean diet, appreciated by those who love natural food, legumes are on my table in every season.

   This is a hot soup to be enjoyed in autumn and winter, with all the taste and nutritional properties of chickpeas. A dish that becomes even richer and more complete if accompanied by rice or pasta. This soup will warm you in the cold months.

## Ingredients

300 g (11 oz) chickpeas
Pinch of baking soda
Sea salt, to taste
1 onion
1 carrot
1 stalk of celery
1 tsp turmeric
Extra virgin olive oil, to
   taste
Rustic bread, to serve

**Serves 4**

## Method

1. Soak the chickpeas overnight with a pinch of baking soda.
2. Drain the chickpeas and pour into a pan of salted water, let them cook for about 1 hour with all the vegetables, previously washed and cut.
3. At the end of the cooking, add the turmeric.
4. Season with extra virgin olive oil and serve with rustic bread.

# DRIED FAVA BEAN PUREE
*Purea di fave*

This recipe is reminiscent of the Sicilian *Macco di fave* (macco comes from the Latin word Maccare, meaning 'crush'), it a delicious bean cream whose ingredients vary in each Sicilian city.

At one time, cooking macco was a very long process. The thick puree, once cooled, could be sliced and consumed by farmers. Nowadays this is a delicious dish, suitable for both adults and children.

You can use it as a nice side dish, or served with pasta it becomes a tasty full dish.

## Ingredients

300 g (11 oz) dried fava beans
Pinch of baking soda
1 sprig parsley
1 potato, peeled
1 red onion, chopped
1 carrot, chopped
Extra virgin olive oil, to taste
Toasted bread, to serve

**Serves 4**

## Method

1. Let the dried Fava beans soak in cold water overnight with a pinch of baking soda.
2. Drain the beans and put them in a pot with salted water, cook for about an hour along with the parsley, potato, onion and carrot, previously washed and cut.
3. When the beans have reached a creamy consistency, turn off the heat.
4. Serve the puree with toasted homemade bread and season with extra virgin olive oil.

# EGG-FREE FRESH PASTA – BASIC RECIPE
*Ricetta base pasta fresca senza uova*

As a women of the south, for me, pasta is strictly dry, prepared with durum wheat semolina. But sometimes, I make an exception for egg-free fresh pasta making it with durum wheat semolina flour, Farro or Kamut flour.

   This is a very easy and quick recipe. You can serve fresh pasta with a simple tomato sauce, pesto or seasonal vegetables.

## Ingredients

200 g (7 oz) organic
   durum wheat flour
Pinch of sea salt
100 g (3½ oz) warm water

**Serves 2**

## Method

1. Pour the flour into a bowl, add a pinch of salt and the water and knead until you have a smooth and elastic texture that will not stick to your hands.
2. Cover with a cloth and let rest in the refrigerator for about 10 minutes.
3. Sprinkle a work surface with a little flour, spread the dough with a rolling pin (if necessary, divide in half) and cut into the desired shape.

# PASTA WITH VEGETABLES AND SCRAMBLED EGGS

*Pasta con verdure e uova strapazzate*

This recipe is suitable for any season. In summer, you can replace the sage and thyme with basil and mint. In spring, you can add fresh peas or zucchini (courgette). Pasta and eggs make this winter variant a complete nutritional dish with a rich taste. Ideal to be served either hot or warm.

## Ingredients

1 stalk of celery
1 clove garlic
Pinch of sea salt
Extra virgin olive oil, to
    taste
4 large eggs
1 tbsp chopped thyme
3 sage leaves
320 g (11 ¼ oz) short
    pasta

**Serves 4**

## Method

1. Cut the celery, slice the garlic and place in a bowl. Season with salt and oil.
2. Beat the eggs with a pinch of salt, add the chopped thyme and sage and scramble the eggs in a frying pan greased with a little extra virgin olive oil.
3. Cook the pasta al dente in boiling salted water. Drain and mix with the vegetables and eggs.

# FENNEL SALAD WITH SICILIAN PISTACHIOS AND SESAME SEEDS

*Insalata di finocchio, pistacchio e sesamo*

This salad celebrates fennel, an often overlooked but very versatile vegetable with a lot of beneficial properties.

This salad, like all those I love to prepare, has crisp ingredients which give a sense of satiety that prevents you eating generous portions in subsequent courses.

The toasted sesame seeds and pistachios give this dish a very strong perfume and taste.

## Ingredients

1 fennel bulb
Extra virgin olive oil, to taste
Sea salt and freshly ground black pepper, to taste
50 g (2 oz) toasted sesame seeds
50 g (2 oz) Parmigiano Reggiano flakes
Sicilian pistachios, chopped, to taste

**Serves 2**

## Method

1. Wash the fennel, remove the hard part of the core and cut into 4 pieces lengthwise (keeping the feet on the core). Slice, rinse and dry using a centrifuge salad spinner or just blot with a clean cloth.
2. In a bowl, pour the oil, salt and pepper and toasted sesame seeds, whisk with a fork and let it sit for about 10 minutes.
3. Pour in the fennel and stir.
4. Add the grated Parmigiano flakes and pistachios and serve.

# PASTA WITH RICOTTA

*Pasta con ricotta*

A delicious, quick and easy dish to prepare, this is really invigorating, especially in winter. One of those comfort foods, born from the ancient peasant tradition, it is a great recipe for those who do not like spending too much time in the kitchen.

## Ingredients

300 g (11 oz) short pasta
300 g (11 oz) fresh ricotta
   (according to your
   taste, sheep or cow's
   ricotta)
Grated Parmigiano
   cheese, to taste
Sea salt and pepper, to
   taste
Chopped parsley, to taste

**Serves 3**

## Method

1. Cook the pasta al dente, in boiling salted water. Drain and save a little of the cooking water.
2. Mix the ricotta with a little Parmigiano, salt and pepper.
3. Add the ricotta to the pasta and mix well.
4. Sprinkle with chopped parsley and serve immediately.

# PASTA AND BEANS
*Pasta e fagioli*

This dish is a classic of the Italian peasant tradition. Pasta and beans were considered the poor man's meat. Today, the percentage of Italians who choose to consume vegetable protein (eliminating or reducing animal protein) has grown considerably, and this dish has been revalued to the status it deserves.

Very popular not only in typical Italian Trattorias but also in starred restaurants, pasta and beans is one of the symbols of Italian home cooking. Every Italian woman will give you her favorite recipe (remember that in Italy, every family has its 'own' version of a recipe). This is one of the most simple and easiest to make.

## Ingredients

500 g (17 oz) dried pinto
   beans
1 tbsp baking soda
A stalk of celery
1 carrot
1 onion
1 shallot
Pinch of sea salt
Pepper, to taste
320 g (11 ¼ oz) short
   pasta

**Serves 4**

## Method

1. The night before, soak the beans in cold water with a tablespoon of baking soda.
2. The next day, rinse the beans thoroughly and cover with water. Cook the beans with the celery, carrot, onion, shallot (all cleaned and cut into rounds) for 50–60 minutes.
3. Halfway through cooking, add the salt, pepper and pasta.
4. Serve warm.

# PASTINA WITH VEGETABLE BROTH

*Pastina con brodo vegetale*

Another staple food of the Italian winter. The pastina in *brodo vegetale* is not only nutritious, but is suitable for small children or for a light dinner that warms you during the cold winters.

The homemade vegetable broth is very easy to prepare and, if made with flavorful vegetables, has a truly unique taste. Also suitable for risotto, it can be prepared in advance and then frozen. My suggestion is that you use it to fill ice cube trays and, once frozen, transfer the cubes into plastic bags for food. In this way, you have broth cubes ready for use whenever needed.

## Ingredients

1 organic onion
1 organic carrot
1 organic celery stalk
1 liter (34 fl oz) water
Sea salt, to taste
300 g (11 oz) pastina
   pasta
Extra virgin olive oil, to
   taste
Parmigiano cheese, to
   taste

**Serves 4**

## Method

1. Peel the onion and cut in half. Peel the carrot and cut into small cubes.
2. Wash and dry the celery and cut into small rounds.
3. Put the water in a large pot, add all the vegetables and cook for 30 minutes over a low heat with the lid on to enhance the cooking of the vegetables.
4. Once done remove the vegetables from the water. Add the salt and pasta, leaving to cook according to the time suggested on the packet.
5. When cooked, add the oil. Sprinkle with grated Parmigiano and serve hot.

# RADICCHIO, FETA AND RUSTIC BREAD SALAD

*Insalata di radicchio, feta e pane rustico*

---

I love this salad for the bright color and the pungent flavor of the radicchio (one of the winter vegetables I love the most), the freshness of the feta and the crunchy hazelnuts.

Rich in many nutrients, it is perfect as a side dish or for a light meal.

## Ingredients

10 radicchio leaves
100 g (3 ½ oz) feta cheese
15 toasted hazelnuts
2 slices rustic bread
2 tbsp extra virgin
　olive oil
Juice of one large lemon
Sea salt and pepper,
　to taste

**Serves 2**

## Method

1. Wash and cut the radicchio. Cut the feta into cubes.
2. Cut half of the hazelnuts coarsely (leave the others whole for decoration).
3. Cut the bread into cubes and toast in the oven.
4. Put all the ingredients together in a bowl.
5. Mix the oil in a bowl with the lemon, salt and pepper and season the salad.
6. Serve immediately.

# PASTA WITH SEITAN RAGU

*Pasta con ragù di Seitan*

This is one of the dishes I most like to prepare in winter and it is very popular amongst my friends.

Seitan sauce (or Ragù) is a sustainable recipe. You don't need to spend hours in the kitchen because it can be made in less than half an hour. The result is a dish rich in nutritional value, recommended for those who love to vary their diet, alternating traditional dishes with delicious and healthy recipes that make your kitchen very personal.

As seitan is very rich in gluten, I prefer to lighten the recipe with gluten-free pasta. For a gluten-free sauce, you can replace the seitan with tofu.

## Ingredients

1 carrot
1 onion
1 stalk of celery
Extra virgin olive oil,
   to taste
150 g (5 oz) seitan (better
   if seitan burger)
250 g (9 oz) tomato sauce
Sea salt, to taste
320 g (11¼ oz) short
   pasta

**Serves 4**

## Method

1. Wash and cut the carrot, onion and celery and cook in a pan with extra virgin olive oil until golden brown.
2. Cut the seitan into cubes and add it to the vegetables when they are almost cooked. Pour the tomato sauce and salt over and cook for 15 minutes over a low heat.
3. Cook the pasta al dente, drain and add to the sauce, mixing everything together.

# SCACCIATA PIE WITH BROCCOLI AND CAULIFLOWER

*Scacciata di broccoli e cavolfiore*

This pie with seasonal vegetables and cheese is a delicious dish to taste freshly baked but it is equally great to eat cold.

This has always been one of the pies that I've loved and it was one of my favorite snacks to take to school after having it for dinner the previous evening. In truth, I liked it even more the next day and still today I appreciate it more after a few hours.

## Ingredients

4 tsp organic instant yeast
500 g (17 oz) wholewheat Farro (or Kamut) flour
Warm water, to taste
Sea salt, to taste
8 tbsp extra virgin olive oil
8 tops of broccoli
8 tops of cauliflower
White pepper, to taste
350 g (12 oz) 'Tuma' Sicilian cheese (or Fontina cheese)

**Serves 6–8**

## Method

1. Mix the yeast with the flour.
2. Add warm water, salt and oil and form a firm but soft dough. Let the mixture rise for 2-3 hours. Roll out the dough on an oiled baking pan.
3. Wash and cut the broccoli and cauliflower and steam cook.
4. Heat a saucepan with 3 tablespoons of extra virgin olive oil and place the broccoli and cauliflower inside, seasoning with salt and white pepper to taste.
5. Cook until the vegetables are browned.
6. Pour the seasoned vegetables into the pan where you placed the dough.
7. Season with the 'Tuma' Sicilian cheese or other high quality soft or semi-soft cheese.
8. Bake at 180°C (350°F/gas 4) for 50 minutes.

# SEITAN STEW

*Spezzatino di Seitan*

Seitan stew is an energy-saver, due to the reduced time cooking. This basic recipe can be replaced or enriched with potatoes, peas, capsicum (bell peppers) or tomatoes, when in season.

Used as a condiment for pasta, it becomes an excellent meal.

## Ingredients

1 leek
2 carrots
3 tbsp extra virgin olive
   oil
Pinch of sea salt
200 g (7 oz) natural
   seitan
1 sprig parsley, chopped

**Serves 4**

## Method

1. Finely chop the leek and dice the carrots.
2. Brown the vegetables for about 20 minutes in a pan heated with oil. If necessary, so as not to dry the vegetables, add a tablespoon of water.
3. Add a pinch of salt and the seitan cut into cubes and stir for 3-4 minutes.
4. Serve hot with chopped parsley.

# USTICHESE LENTILS
*Lenticchie alla Ustichese*

Ustica is a small island off the Sicilian archipelago where they cultivate a small and fine lentil –the Slow Food Presidium. Particularly tender, when cooked it gives off a delicious aroma. Its organoleptic characteristics are derived from the Mediterranean climate and the volcanic soil in which it grows.

Rich in iron and proteins, the lentil is a legume that never fails on the Italian table and is a perfect meat substitute.

In summer, you can add zucchini (courgette), fresh tomatoes and basil to this dish.

## Ingredients

500 g (17 oz) lentils
1 onion
1 clove garlic
1 carrot
7 sun-dried tomatoes
Chili, to taste
Pinch of sea salt, to taste
Sage leaves, to taste
Extra virgin olive oil,
   to taste
Rustic bread, to serve

**Serves 4–6**

## Method

1. Wash the lentils, put them in a pot and cover with cold water.
2. Cut the onion, garlic, carrot and sun-dried tomatoes and add to lentils.
3. Cook for 25 minutes. Add the chili, sea salt and sage to taste and cook for other 5 minutes.
4. Serve with rustic bread.

# VALDOSTANA SALAD

*Insalata Valdostana*

---

This salad releases the flavors of the Valle D'Aosta region (in north Italy), and is great to open a meal.

A concentrate of very strong flavors that do not conflict with each other but, on the contrary, enhance each other.

## Ingredients

200 g (7 oz) valeriana leaves (or rocket (arugula))
10 radicchio leaves
100 g (3½ oz) Fontina cheese
100 g (3½ oz) shelled walnuts or almonds
Extra virgin olive oil, to taste
Sea salt, to taste
Balsamic vinegar, to taste

**Serves 2**

## Method

1. Wash and dry the valeriana and radicchio leaves, cut coarsely and place in a bowl.
2. Addt he Fontina, cut into cubes, and the walnuts, broken in half. Season with a little oil, salt and pepper and a generous splash of balsamic vinegar.

# WINTER SALAD
*Insalata invernale*

The artichokes in this salad are a very rich source of potassium and phosphorus, and like the radicchio, also calcium and iron.

The Modena cream balsamic vinegar and walnuts (if possible, choose local dried ones) are the key to a salad that, in my house, in winter, is very much in demand.

## Ingredients

10 artichoke hearts
2 fennel bulbs
10 radicchio leaves
Extra virgin olive oil,
   to taste
Sea salt, to taste
Pepper, to taste
20 walnuts
1 tbsp Modena cream
   balsamic vinegar

**Serves 2**

## Method

1. Clean the artichokes, remove the heart and steam cook them for 30 minutes.
2. Slice the fennel and cut the radicchio and wash both in cold water. Dry the vegetables with a clean cloth (or with a centrifuge salad spinner).
3. Place the oil, salt and pepper in a small bowl and emulsify with a fork (or a small whisk).
4. Roughly chop the walnuts.
5. Place all ingredients in a large bowl and mix, adding another tablespoon of oil and vinegar to taste.

# CHOCOLATE SALAMI
*Salame di cioccolato*

Chocolate salami reminds me of my childhood and even now I consider it one of my favorite desserts. You only have to try one slice and you'll be craving more. The unique thing about this recipe is the Marsala dessert Sicilian wine which gives a special and delicious taste to the dessert. If you prefer, you can replace it with another fine Sicilian dessert wine like Passito di Pantelleria.

## Ingredients

150 g (5 oz) dry digestive cookies, palm oil free
4 tbsp raw sugar
50 g (2 oz) cocoa powder
100 g (3½ oz) chopped roasted hazelnuts
100 g (3½ oz) roasted pistachios
1 large egg
300 g (11 oz) 70% dark chocolate
150 g (5 oz) butter
2 tbsp Marsala Sicilian wine dessert or Rum (to be avoided if the dessert is made for children)

**Serves 6–8**

## Method

1. Chop the cookies and add them to the sugar, cocoa powder, hazelnuts and pistachios.
2. Lightly beat the egg with a fork and add to the cookie mixture.
3. Melt the chocolate in a double boiler with the butter. When cool add the Marsala wine and stir into the cookie mixture.
4. Pour the dough onto parchment paper, sprinkle with more cocoa powder and work it into a sausage shape. Keep the dough wrapped in parchment paper and store in the refrigerator for 4–5 hours.
5. Remove the salami from the refrigerator 20 minutes before serving.
6. You can present it in its entirety on a serving dish (adding, if necessary, another dusting of cocoa powder) or serve it sliced.

# HOT SPICY CHOCOLATE
*Cioccolata calda speziata*

If you are accustomed to shop bought hot chocolate, rich in sugars and thickeners, this recipe might seem trivial. In truth, the traditional hot chocolate, consumed by the Aztecs (inventors of the chocolate and cocoa) is liquid prepared with water and is sugar free. It is a drink for connoisseurs. My version, made with Modica Aztec chocolate, contains the sugars already present in the chocolate (you can add a few tablespoons of raw brown sugar) and the delicious taste of cinnamon that fits perfectly with the cocoa. You can choose other spices such as pepper, ginger or nutmeg as well.

## Ingredients

200 ml (7 fl oz) water
1 heaped tsp raw cocoa
    powder
150 g (5 oz) Modica
    chocolate (or high
    quality dark chocolate
    70% or 80%)
ground cinnamon, to
    taste

**Serves 2**

## Method

1. Pour the water and cocoa powder into a saucepan and simmer for 3 minutes.
2. Break the chocolate into small pieces and mix in the liquid for a minute with a stick blender away from the heat.
3. Add the cinnamon, put back on the heat for 2 minutes and serve.

# CHOCOLATE TRUFFLES

*Tartufi di cioccolato*

Chocolate truffles are a pearl of Turin pastry. They have a delicious sweetness when dissolved in your mouth, and you can savor the taste of every single ingredient. This homemade recipe is perfect for an easy and refined dessert.

## Ingredients

250 g (9 oz) fresh cream
50 g (2 oz) butter
200 g (7 oz) 70% dark chocolate
200 g (7 oz) milk chocolate
150 g (5 oz) toasted and chopped hazelnuts

**Makes about 50–60 truffles**

## Method

1. Heat the cream on the stove with the butter, without boiling the mix.
2. Add the chocolate and stir the mix vigorously until it has melted.
3. Add 50 g (2 oz) of the toasted and chopped hazelnuts.
4. Pour the mixture into a bowl and allow to cool to room temperature, then store in the fridge for at least 2 hours.
5. When the ganache has reached the right consistency, take a small amount of dough and form it into a ball.
6. Roll it in the hazelnuts and repeat until you've made enough truffles.
7. Keep the truffles in the fridge and pull them out just before serving.

# PEAR AND RICOTTA CUPS

*Coppette di pere con ricotta*

Pears are a very versatile fruit, especially in the preparation of desserts. This is a very quick idea, perfect to serve at the end of a meal or for an afternoon snack.

Also in this recipe, I suggest raisin as sweetener, if you are not yet accustomed to a less sweet flavor, you can add a tablespoon of honey.

## Ingredients

2 tbsp raisins (palm oil free)
2 tbsp Marsala dessert wine
3 pears
2 tbsp honey
Juice of 1 red orange
150 g (5 oz) ricotta, drained
Ground cinnamon, to taste

**Serves 4**

## Method

1. Wash the raisins and soak in warm water with the Marsala.
2. Peel the pears, cut into cubes and place in a saucepan with the honey and orange juice. Cook over a medium heat for 10 minutes and then let cool.
3. Mix the pear sauce with the ricotta and drained raisins and blend in a mixer at full power.
4. Spread the cream into 4 glass cups, sprinkle with cinnamon and serve immediately.

# SUGAR-FREE MOIST CHOCOLATE CAKE
*Torta morbida di cioccolato senza zucchero*

This cake just calls on the natural sweetness of its ingredients. The result is a moist cake, just sweet enough with rich chocolate flavor. Italian Farro flour gives the cake a perfect consistency (you can find it in the best Italian food shops or you can replace it with Kamut flour).

This is a cake that will be much appreciated by connoisseurs of chocolate. Don't skimp on the quality of chocolate, this is the key to the recipe. A good extra light virgin olive oil gives the right softness, making this cake, with an Italian twist, delicious and healthy.

## Ingredients

2 tbsp raisins
2 tbsp dried apricots
150 g (5 oz) high quality 60% bitter dark chocolate
100 g (3½ oz) high quality 70% bitter dark chocolate
2 large eggs
2 tbsp Greek yogurt
4 tbsp extra virgin olive oil or 6 tbsp organic cold pressed sunflower oil
Pinch of sea salt
250 g (9 oz) wholewheat Farro flour, sifted
1 tsp organic baking powder, sifted
1 tsp vanilla 'Bourbon' powder

## Method

1. Preheat the oven to180°C (350°F/gas 4).
2. Wash and dry the fruit, blend at maximum power and set aside.
3. Melt the chocolate in a double boiler (or a thick-bottomed pan) and, once removed from the heat, allow to cool.
4. Beat the eggs vigorously. Add the yogurt, oil, a pinch of salt and stir to combine the ingredients.
5. Add the first 100 g (3½ oz) of flour, sifted with baking powder. Once mixed with the liquid ingredients, add the remaining flour, with the vanilla, stirring quickly. Finally add the raisin and apricot puree.
6. Pour in the chocolate and mix the dough without working it too much, otherwise your cake will not become soft.
7. Lined a mold with baking paper, pour in the mix and bake for 25-30 minutes.

**Serves 6–8**

# WINTER MACEDONIA OR FRUIT SALAD

*Macedonia invernale o insalata di frutta*

In winter, rather than fruit colors or varieties, I play with flavors. Bananas, rich in potassium and magnesium, match well with apples and kiwis. The blood orange juice mixed with malt and just warmed up, is the delicious twist that gives a particular sweetness to the fruit salad.

## Ingredients

2 bananas
2 red apples
2 kiwis
Juice of 1 lemon
A handful of walnuts
A handful of chopped
  orange zest
Juice of 1 red orange
1 tbsp rice malt

**Serves 2**

## Method

1. Cut the bananas, red apples and kiwis and place in a bowl.
2. Sprinkle the fruit with lemon juice to prevent browning.
3. Add the coarsely chopped walnuts and orange zest.
4. In a pan, mix the orange juice with malt for 2 minutes and pour over the salad.

SPRING

# ASPARAGUS AND ZUCCHINI CAKE

*Torta di asparagi e zucchine*

Spring is asparagus season, time for outdoor meals and recipes to be enjoyed cold for picnics or brunch.

This is one of my most popular savory dishes with wild asparagus. Not always easy to find, wild asparagus is as precious as its distinctive flavor.

## Ingredients

4 zucchini (courgettes) (3, if large)
1 onion
15 asparagus
Sea salt and white pepper, to taste
2 large eggs
75 g (3½ oz) grated Parmigiano cheese
Extra virgin olive oil, to taste
1 sheet puff pastry

**Serves 4–6**

## Method

1. Wash and slice the zucchini, peel the onion and steam cook all for about 15 minutes.
2. Clean the asparagus, removing the ends and blanch in salted water for 10 minutes. Once cooked, mix all the vegetables in the pan and season with salt.
3. In a bowl, beat the eggs and season with salt, pepper and Parmigiano.
4. Roll out the pastry on a greased baking sheet or covered with parchment paper. Add the vegetables and cover with the beaten eggs
5. Bake, in preheated oven, for 15–20 minutes at 180°C (350°F/gas 4).

# ASPARAGUS WITH CRUMBLE

*Asparagi con briciole di frolla salata*

Breadsticks (grissini) are one of the most celebrated Italian specialties (you can find them in the best Italian food shops). These loaves of bread stretched and crisp, born in Turin, have different forms, according to the various regions of Italy. In Sicily, for example, they are covered with sesame seeds.

The sesame grissini crumbs are the added value of this very simple but tasty recipe. A time-saving and sustainable idea, best served as an appetizer or side dish.

## Ingredients

1 bunch of asparagus
Extra virgin olive oil, to taste
Sea salt and white pepper, to taste
6 grissini
50 g (2 oz) toasted almonds

**Serves 4**

## Method

1. In a pot, boil salted water. Wash the asparagus and remove the harder end part of the stem.
2. When the water starts to boil, add the asparagus and let cook for 5 minutes.
3. Drain and place on a baking sheet, covered with parchment paper. Drizzle with olive oil, salt and pepper.
4. In a blender, put the grissini, add the almonds and extra virgin olive oil to taste. Blend until you have coarse crumbs.
5. Pour the crumble on the asparagus and cook in a preheated oven at 180°C (350°F/gas 4) for 10 minutes.

# BAKED PENNE WITH CHEESES AND ZUCCHINI

*Pennei al forno con formaggio e zucchine*

Baked pasta or Pasta al forno is a classic comfort food. Every Italian family has its own recipe and every Italian mother believes to have the best. At one time, much more than today, baked pasta dishes were rich in ingredients, especially meat.

A vegetarian version with fresh seasonal vegetables and cheese is a good, lighter but equally tasty alternative.

## Ingredients

1 onion
Extra virgin olive oil,
  to taste
1 carrot
2 zucchini (courgette)
50 ml (2 oz) water
100 g (3½ oz) butter
75 g (3 oz) white Farro flour
  (or brown rice flour),
  sifted
75 ml (3 fl oz) organic milk
Grated nutmeg, to taste
Pinch of sea salt
Pepper, to taste
50 g (2 oz) grated
  Parmigiano
320 g (11¼ oz) Penne or
  other short pasta
100 g (3½ oz) Fontina, cut
  into cubes

## Method

1. Peel the onion, chop and cook on a low heat for 10 minutes in a pan with a little olive oil.
2. Wash and cut the carrot into cubes. Wash the zucchini and cut into cubes. Add both to the onion. Add water and let cook for 15 minutes, covering the pan with a lid.
3. In a saucepan, melt the butter, add the flour, stirring with a whisk to avoid lumps.
4. Add the milk little by little, stirring constantly. Add nutmeg, salt and pepper and continue cooking for another 5-6 minutes until the béchamel sauce is not too thick.
5. Off the heat, add the Parmigiano cheese.
6. Cook the pasta in boiling salted water then drain.
7. Mix the pasta with the béchamel sauce, Fontina cheese, vegetables and place on a greased baking sheet.
8. Bake at 180°C (350°F/gas 4) for 10-15 minutes. Serve hot.

**Serves 4**

# BREADED TOFU STICKS WITH ASPARAGUS AND PARMIGIANO SAUCE

*Bastoncini di Tofu panato con asparagi e crema di Parmigiano*

Thanks to this simple dish, some of my friends have changed their minds on the pleasantness of tofu. Tofu has a neutral flavor which according to some, is its weak point. On the contrary, I think it's its strong point because it allows you to experiment with various seasonings.

The breaded tofu sticks, accompanied by a delicate Parmigiano sauce, become a crisp and tasty idea that will appeal to children.

## Ingredients

10 asparagus spears
Pinch of sea salt
100 g (3½ oz) natural tofu
60 g (2 oz) brown rice
  flour
1 large beaten egg
60 g (2 oz) breadcrumbs
Extra virgin olive oil,
  to taste
100 g (3½ oz) grated
  Parmigiano cheese
60 ml (2 oz) organic rice
  drink milk (or cow's
  milk)
Grated nutmeg or white
  pepper, to taste

**Serves 2**

## Method

1. Wash and clean the asparagus, removing the hardest part at the end and blanch in salted water for about 10minutes (cooking should be al dente). Drain and set aside.
2. Drain the tofu and cut into strips. Prepare one bowl containing the flour, one bowl containing beaten egg with a pinch of salt and one bowl containing the breadcrumbs.
3. Dip each stick of tofu, in sequence, in the flour, egg and then breadcrumbs. In an oiled skillet, cook the tofu sticks for a few minutes until they are golden.
4. Arrange the sticks on a plate with paper towels and set aside.
5. In a saucepan, melt the Parmigiano with the milk, until it becomes a fluid cream. Remove from heat, add the nutmeg or pepper according to your taste.
6. In a serving dish, place the asparagus and tofu and season with the Parmigiano sauce, prepared just before serving.

# BARLEY AND FARRO WARM SALAD
*Insalata tiepida di Farro e Orzo*

Spring is an uncertain time of year. The temperatures undergo changes and, especially in the first part of the season there are still some cool days that necessitate hot meals or, at least, lukewarm.

This warm salad is a perfect compromise and a tasty way to enjoy, among other things, the numerous benefits of two noble cereals – barley and farro.

The quantity of farro and barley used in this recipe require roughly the same cooking time but this may vary according to the packet you purchased.

## Ingredients

150 g (4½ oz) barley
100 g (3½ oz) whole
  wheat farro
2 carrots
150 g (4½ oz) fresh peas
1 leek
1 stalk of celery
500 ml (14 fl oz) water
Sea salt, to taste
Extra virgin olive oil, to
  taste

**Serves 2**

## Method

1. Rinse the barley and farro in cold water and drain.
2. Peel the carrots and cut into cubes. Clean the peas. Clean and slice the leeks. Wash and chop the celery.
3. Cook the farro, barley, carrots, peas, leek and celery in boiling salted water for 25-30 minutes (or according to the time indicated on the package), covering with a lid.
4. Drain the salad. Allow to cool and drizzle with extra virgin olive oil.

# BROWN RICE WITH SICILIAN TOMATO PESTO

*Riso integrale con pesto Siciliano di pomodoro*

The crunchiness of rice meets the strong and unique flavor of Sicilian pesto. A few good ingredients give birth to a sauce that I love to prepare at the end of spring when the smell of tomatoes from my garden, and the first leaves of fresh basil, fill my kitchen. Almonds toasted just before the preparation of the sauce are the added value that makes the difference.

## Ingredients

200 g (7 oz) brown rice
10 sun-dried tomatoes
1 red capsicum (bell pepper)
5 toasted almonds
1 tbsp tomato sauce
6 basil leaves
Pinch of sea salt
Extra virgin olive oil, to taste

**Serves 2**

## Method

1. Cook the rice in boiling salted water. Drain and set aside.
2. Coarsely cut the sun-dried tomatoes, capsicum and almonds and mix in a blender with the remaining ingredients.
3. In a bowl, put the rice and mix with the tomato pesto. Sprinkle with extra virgin olive oil to taste.

# BROWN RICE WITH VEGETABLES AND CREAMY TOFU

*Riso integrale con verdure e tofu cremoso*

The spring cuisine anticipates the tastes of summer dishes. It is a season that, especially in the second part, offers colorful vegetables, rich in vitamins useful for the body to deal with the summer heat.

   This dish, a source of fiber and vitamins, is ideal for a light, nutritious meal. Creamy tofu (available in the best supermarkets and health food stores), rich in protein, is the key idea of this recipe.

## Ingredients

200 g (7 oz) brown rice
100 g (3½ oz) fresh
   green beans
1 clove of garlic
4 carrots
Extra virgin olive oil,
   to taste plus 1 tbsp
   for the tofu sauce
200 g (7 oz) creamy
   tofu
Sea salt and pepper,
   to taste
Sprig of parsley

**Serves 2**

## Method

1. Cook the brown rice in boiling salted water until  al dente, drain and set aside (for cooking times, follow the instructions on the packet).
2. Steam the green beans in salted water for 20 minutes.
3. Check the green beans then drain and cut them into pieces.
4. Peel the garlic and cut finely. Wash the carrots and cut into rounds.
5. In a skillet, brown the garlic with the oil. Remove the garlic, add the vegetables and sauté for 10 minutes. Season with salt and pepper.
6. In a bowl, mix the tofu with a tablespoon of oil and chopped parsley, add salt and pepper and mix. (The same method can be followed with natural tofu but, in this case, to obtain a creamy sauce, you'll have to blend the tofu with 2 tbsp olive oil and milk or soy cream).
7. Place the rice in a serving dish, add the vegetables and mix with the tofu sauce. Serve warm or cold.

# BRUSCHETTA WITH ASPARAGUS AND CHERRY TOMATOES

*Bruschetta con asparagi e pomodorini*

The smell of rustic bread and still warm, fresh and crispy vegetables (best if freshly picked) plus good olive oil are the best way to enjoy this dish.

I like to eat asparagus in various ways, even just blanched and served with an excellent quality oil. In this case, the freshly harvested garlic gives a lively flavor and enhances the rest of the ingredients.

## Ingredients

200 g (7 oz) asparagus
   cut in half lengthwise
3 tbsp extra virgin olive
   oil
Pinch of sea salt
250 g (9 oz) cherry
   tomatoes cut in half
1 ciabatta or rustic
   bread, cut into 12 slices
1 clove garlic, cut in half
2 tbsp Parmigiano flakes

**Serves 4–6**

## Method

1. Heat a skillet over a high heat. Brush the asparagus with 1 tablespoon extra virgin olive oil, add a pinch of salt and cook in the pan, along with the tomatoes for about 10 minutes. Turn occasionally until they are slightly charred. Remove from the heat and keep warm.
2. Heat the slices of bread, rub one side of each slice with the garlic and transfer them on to a platter.
3. Arrange the asparagus and cherry tomatoes on the bread. Drizzle with the remaining olive oil and, if desired, a sprinkling of Parmigiano.

# CHICKPEA-BARLEY SALAD WITH TOMATO AND ALMOND PESTO

*Insalata di ceci e orzo con pomodori e pesto di mandorle*

This recipe retains all the flavor of the pesto with a Sicilian twist. It particularly brings out all its flavors and creamy texture when served with lukewarm barley and with a little oil added just before serving.

## Ingredients

200 g (7 oz) barley
100 g (3½ oz) organic
   canned chickpeas
5 sun-dried tomatoes
10 date tomatoes
10 desalted capers
5 fresh oregano leaves
5 basil leaves
50 g (2 oz) fresh ricotta
6 tbsp extra virgin olive
   oil
Pinch of sea salt
White pepper, to taste

**Serves 2**

## Method

1. Wash and drain the barley. Cook in boiling salted water for the time listed on the packaging.
2. Drain the chickpeas and set aside.
3. In a blender, mix the sun-dried tomatoes with all the remaining the ingredients, and blend until you have a thick and creamy pesto.
4. In a bowl, mix the barley with the chickpeas and pesto, stirring well to combine ingredients. Serve.

# CREAMY PEA SOUP

*Zuppa di piselli cremosa*

Fresh peas are precious. I buy them from a lady who cultivates a small piece of countryside with a truly moving dedication. Of course, their flavor is totally different from the peas bought at the supermarket, especially those frozen (which are very high in pesticides). If nature has given peas a very short season it is nonsense that we insist on having them all year round.

It may be useful, if desired, to freeze fresh peas when you have a good supply during the summer. But if you fancy a really tasty pea soup, go in search of fresh green peas from the farms in your area. You will not regret it.

## Ingredients

3 spring onions
  (scallions)
500 g (17 oz) fresh peas
Sea salt, to taste
Extra virgin olive oil,to
  taste
1 sprig of mint

**Serves 4**

## Method

1. Wash the spring onion, peel and cut into cubes.
2. Wash the peas and cook in salted water with the spring onions for about 25 minutes (time cooking varies according to the size of the fresh peas).
3. Once cooked, puree the peas in a blender, adding 2 tablespoons of olive oil and, if necessary, water to taste.
4. Season with a drizzle of extra virgin olive oil and a sprig of mint.
5. Serve immediately.

# EGGS AL TEGAMINO

*Uova al tegamino*

One of the simplest (but not trivial) recipes provides an opportunity to focus on a food that, at times, is mistreated. Some people cook eggs when they have little time or when there are few ingredients in the pantry, as if they were a stop gap. On the contrary, eggs are an ancient, valuable food if taken in moderation and, especially, if selected carefully. Find fresh organic free range eggs, coming from local certified farms and you'll taste the difference to eggs sold in the supermarket.

In this case, the color and taste of a simple *al tegamino* fried egg makes all the difference. Eating an egg from a healthy and happy hen is not a substitute but a real luxury.

## Ingredients

1 tbsp extra virgin olive oil
2 large eggs
Sea salt and pepper, to taste

**Serves 2**

## Method

1. Heat a non stick skillet and add the olive oil.
2. Separate the egg whites from the egg yolks and place in two separate bowls.
3. Pour the egg whites into the skillet and cook for 2 minutes.
4. Add the egg yolks and cook for another two minutes (until the yolk is soft inside).
5. Season with salt and pepper to taste. Serve immediately.

# GRILLED VEGETABLES IN PUFF PASTRY
*Sfoglia di verdure grigliate*

Usually used as an excellent side dish, grilled vegetables are a classic of the spring and summer table. Used as a filling for a puff pastry they become a very tasty appetizer or snack, ideal to also serve in single portions.

## Ingredients

3 zucchini (courgettes)
3 capsicum (bell pepper)
3 eggplants (aubergines)
6 tbsp extra virgin olive
  oil
Sea salt, to taste
Balsamic vinegar, to
  taste
1 sheet puff pastry (palm
  oil free)

**Serves 4–6**

## Method

1. Wash and dry the zucchini, capsicum and eggplant and cut into slices, cubes or strips, as you wish (for single portions, it is preferable to cut the vegetables into small pieces). Brush the vegetables with the oil.
2. Grill the vegetables on a hot plate, turning and adding salt halfway through cooking.
3. Place the vegetables in a bowl. Add the remaining oil, a pinch of salt and balsamic vinegar. Stir and set aside.
4. Place a sheet of puff pastry on a baking sheet, covered with parchment paper. With the tines of a fork prick the surface and cook in a preheated oven at 180°C (350°F/gas 4) for about 10 minutes or before the edges of the pastry start to brown.
5. Pull the pastry out of the oven, arrange the vegetables on top and cook on the top shelf of the oven for another 5 minutes. If necessary, before serving, brush the vegetables with oil. Serve warm.

# MEDITERRANEAN SPAGHETTI
*Spaghetti Mediterranei*

The Mediterranean diet, not only focuses on food but on the philosophy of life behind this diet. Seasonality, simplicity and variety of ingredients are the most common principles but basically there is the pleasure of eating and not just to satisfy a basic need. Usually, for Italians, this means getting together around a table and enjoying their meal, be it a salad, a sandwich or a pasta dish. This recipe celebrates the Mediterranean philosophy of good food with the seasonal vegetables of spring as it increasingly heads towards summer.

## Ingredients

2 zucchini (courgette)
150 g (5 oz) cherry
  tomatoes
1 capsicum (bell pepper)
1 clove garlic
1 sprig basil
1 sprig parsley
3 mint leaves
3 sage leaves
1 tbsp dried oregano
Extra virgin olive oil, to
  taste
Sea salt and white
  pepper, to taste
320 g (11¼ oz)
  wholewheat pasta

**Serves 4**

## Method

1. Wash the zucchini, cut into slices and cook in salted water for about 1–5 minutes, cooking until al dente. Once cooked, pour the zucchini in to a pan.
2. Add the tomatoes (washed and cut in half); capsicum (washed and cut into slices); garlic, peeled and crushed; the basil leaves, parsley, mint and sage (washed and coarsely cut).
3. Add the oregano, extra virgin olive oil, salt and pepper. Mix the ingredients and cook for 10–12 minutes.
4. Cook the pasta until al dente in boiling salted water. Drain and stir through the sauce.

# SIMPLY BURRATA

*Burrata*

---

Puglia (Southern Italy) is a stunning land, rich in culinary treasures. Among them, the burrata (pronounced boor-rah-tah) is one of the best-known assets and appreciated by all lovers of fine Italian cuisine.

The name is already very evocative and in sound, reminds the speaker of the creaminess of butter (*burro* is the Italian for 'butter'). A true masterpiece of a cheese that should be enjoyed at maximum freshness, accompanied with a fresh salad, a drizzle of extra virgin olive oil, seasonal vegetables and rustic, freshly baked bread.

Burrata was born in the Apulian city of Andria in the early 1900. It soon spread throughout Apulia, then in the Basilicata bordering region with gastronomic traditions similar to those of Puglia. Unfortunately, unlike the mozzarella, it has very limited availability (it must be consumed within a maximum of 2 days) and, therefore, abroad is known only by true connoisseurs.

## Ingredients

150 g (5 oz) burrata
high quality extra virgin
  olive oil, to taste

**Serves 2**

## Method

1. Pull the burrata out of the fridge 20 minutes before serving and place on a serving dish.
2. Serve with excellent extra virgin olive oil. If you wish, you can add dried Sicilian oregano.
3. Serve with seasonal vegetables.

# MINESTRONE

*Minestrone*

---

One of the oldest recipes of the Italian poor cuisine, born in northern Italy in the homes of peasants.

In 1891, Pellegrino Artusi, author of the most famous Italian cookbook, *The Science of Cooking and the Art of Eating Well*, included this recipe in his book, giving minestrone the relevance usually reserved for much more high-standing dishes.

There is no single recipe, because this dish varies according to seasonal ingredients. Usually, in the spring, minestrone has a greater wealth of vegetables and, for this, I think it is much more delicious to enjoy it in this season.

## Ingredients

100 g (3½ oz) fresh peas
100 g (3½ oz) beans
3 carrots
1 stalk of celery
1 bunch of parsley
4 potatoes
1 L (35 fl oz) vegetable broth
2 tbsp extra virgin olive oil
1 shallot
Pinch of sea salt

**Serves 4**

## Method

1. Shell the peas and beans, wash them and set aside.
2. Wash the carrots, cut the ends off and slice. Wash the celery, remove the filaments and slice. Wash the parsley leaves, pat dry with paper towel and chop. Peel the potatoes and cut into cubes.
3. Heat the broth.
4. In a large pot put the oil and coarsely chopped shallot. Cook over a low heat until it takes on a golden color. Add the peas, beans and other vegetables.
5. Cook for 5 minutes over a high heat, stirring constantly.
6. Add the vegetable broth and a pinch of salt and cook for 45 minutes over a low heat.
7. Serve with a drizzle of olive oil.

# ORECCHIETTE WITH CAPER PESTO AND ROCKET (ARAGULA)

*Orecchiette con pesto di capperi e rucola*

In spring and summer I love to prepare various types of pesto, simply because these seasons provide a variety of ingredients with which you can create different combinations.

Caper and rocket (aragula) pesto is perfect with dry orecchiette for a combination of rough textures and strong flavors.

## Ingredients

100 g (3½ oz) desalted capers
A bunch of rocket (aragula)
1 tbsp dried oregano
1 tbsp dried chili
1 tbsp Parmigiano
Extra virgin olive oil, to taste
Pinch of sea salt
320 g (11¼ oz) dried orecchiette pasta

**Serves 4**

## Method

1. In a blender, put the capers, rocket, oregano, dried chili, Parmigiano cheese, extra virgin olive oil, a pinch of salt and blend for 1 or 2 minutes to get a coarse pesto, not too creamy.
2. Cook the orecchiette until al dente in boiling salted water. Drain and mix through the pesto.

# PASTA AND CHICKPEAS

*Pasta e ceci*

This is a recipe as old as Italian cuisine itself, it is also born from the peasant tradition. You can enrich this dish according to your taste or, more simply, as I like to do, just enjoy excellent quality chickpeas. Often, many of us have little time in the kitchen and in this case you can prepare a good plate of pasta with organic chickpeas from a glass jar (this is preferable packaging because it allows you to test the product with sight).

## Ingredients

200 g (7 oz) organic chickpeas in a glass jar

1 carrot

1 onion

1 stalk celery

Extra virgin olive oil, to taste

1 clove garlic

1 ladle water

Sea salt and pepper, to taste

320 g (11¼ oz) cornflour penne

A sprig of parsley, chopped

**Serves 4**

## Method

1. Drain and rinse the chickpeas under cold running water and set aside.
2. Finely chop the carrot, onion and celery. In a large skillet or pot put a tablespoon of olive oil and cook the chopped carrots, onions and celery with a clove of garlic.
3. As soon as they are golden, add the chickpeas and cover with a ladle of water. Season with salt and pepper and cook over a low heat for about 10 minutes.
4. Cook the pasta until al dente in boiling salted water. Add to the chickpeas and mix over a low heat for a few minutes. Garnish with parsley to serve.

# SPRING SAVORY SMALL PIE
*Tortine salate*

These savory pies are an example of how you can integrate complete ingredients into a single dish. Perfect for a brunch, a picnic, as an appetizer or for a snack, they are ideal enjoyed warm or cold.

## Ingredients

2 onions
3 potatoes
100 g (3½ oz) fresh peas
1 bunch of parsley
150 g (5 oz) white Farro flour
15 g (½ oz) organic baking powder
1 tbsp Parmigiano, grated
Pinch of sea salt
2 tbsp extra virgin olive oil
6 eggs

**Serves 6**

## Method

1. Peel the onions and potatoes and steam cook them.
2. Wash the fresh peas and parsley and steam cook them together for 25 minutes with a pinch of salt.
3. Mash the potatoes through a sieve. Add flour, baking powder, Parmigiano and olive oil. Knead for a few minutes to compact the dough.
4. Roll out the dough into 4 or 6 (depending on their size) muffin molds, greased and floured.
5. Pour over the peas, onions and 1 egg yolk for each mold. Season with a sprinkle of olive oil and bake at 180°C (350°F/gas 4).

# PASTA WITH PEAS AND ASPARAGUS SAUCE

*Pasta con salsa di piselli e asparagi*

Pesto is a sauce made with raw ingredients but, in the spring, I make an exception. On days when I am fortunate enough to have plenty of peas and asparagus I try to exploit these allies in every possible way.

This pesto is delicious, fragrant and just as tasty as the traditional recipe.

## Ingredients

100 g (3½ oz) asparagus
300 g (11 oz) fresh peas
1 spring onion (scallion)
100 g (3½ oz) cow's milk ricotta cheese
50 g (2 oz) Parmigiano, grated
2 mint leaves
5 basil leaves
1 tbsp toasted almonds
Extra virgin olive oil
Pinch of sea salt
320 g (11¼ oz) short pasta

**Serves 4**

## Method

1. Clean the asparagus and boil in salted water for 10-12 minutes. Drain and set aside.
2. Clean the fresh peas and cook in salted water with the spring onion (washed, cleaned and cut into cubes) for about 25-30 minutes, according to the size of the peas (fresh peas require a cooking time of at least 30 minutes. Pre-cooked or frozen peas may have a lower cooking times). Drain and let cool.
3. In a blender add the asparagus, peas and the remaining ingredients. Blend until frothy, adding oil if necessary.
4. Cook the pasta until al dente in boiling salted water. Drain and stir through the sauce.

# SPRING SOUP
*Zuppa di primavera*

---

Do not hesitate to consume soups in the spring and summer, several times a week. They are a blessing and help to purify.

I made this recipe with barley but feel free to alternate with farro, brown rice or kamut. All these cereals are rich in fiber and nutrients.

## Ingredients

200 g (7 oz) pearl barley
1 ½ L (3 pt) cold water
1 leek
2 zucchini (courgettes)
1 carrot
3 cherry tomatoes
Sea salt to taste
4 tbsp extra virgin olive
  oil

**Serves 2**

## Method

1. Soak the barley for two hours in warm water, then drain and rinse well under running water. Wash and slice all the vegetables.
2. Transfer the barley into a pot, add the cold water, leek, zucchini, carrot and tomatoes.
3. Add the salt and bring to a boil, lower the heat and cook the barley and vegetables for 20 minutes until al dente.
4. Stir, season with a little olive oil and serve.

# TOMATO FRITTATA
*Frittata di pomodoro*

Small frittatas with tomato sauce were the snack that my mother made for us girls to take to school with the first tomatoes of the season.

The frittata was cooked in the oven, a tradition handed down from mother to daughter. Best to enjoy freshly baked they are also nice cold, cut into cubes and served as appetizer like Spanish tapas.

## Ingredients

4 large eggs
Pinch of sea salt
White pepper, to taste
50 ml (2 fl oz) organic milk
Extra virgin olive oil, to taste
50 g (2 oz) brown rice flour
1 tbsp instant yeast
2 tbsp Parmigiano cheese, grated
15 dates or cherry tomatoes
10 basil leaves
5 mint leaves

**Makes 4**

## Method

1. Beat the eggs with a pinch of salt and pepper. Add the milk, oil, flour, baking powder, Parmigiano and stir with a fork to mix all ingredients.
2. Wash, dry and cut the tomatoes in half. Wash, dry and coarsely chop the basil and mint and add to the frittata dough.
3. Cover 4 mini molds (10 cm/4 in) with removable bottoms with parchment paper.
4. Pour the mixture into each mold.
5. Bake at 180°C (350°F/gas 4) for about 15 minutes.

# PANINI WITH MELTED CHEESE, SEASONAL VEGETABLES AND VEGGIE WURSTEL

*Panini con formaggio fuso, verdure di stagione e wurstel vegetariani*

Vegetarian sausages, generally made from a blend of seasoned cereal and vegetable protein, are perfect meat-substitutes.

This is a healthy sandwich, ideal for a meal in the office. Seasonal vegetables give a touch of freshness perfect for a sandwich that's crispy and full of flavor.

## Ingredients

2 eggplants (aubergines) (1 if large)
1 capsicum (bell pepper), yellow or red
2 zucchini (courgettes) (1 if large)
1 potato
1 clove of garlic
Extra virgin olive oil, to taste
Sea salt, to taste
Rosemary and oregano, to taste
2 veggie wurstel, palm oil free
100 g (3½ oz) Fontina, Crescenza or other soft/ semi-soft cheese, cut into cubes
2 rustic country style slices of bread

**Serves 2**

## Method

1. Clean all vegetables, dry them and cut into chunks.
2. In a skillet, heat the oil and brown the garlic. Remove the garlic, add the potato and pepper (which have a longer cooking time than the eggplant and zucchini). Stir often and cook for about 10 minutes on low heat, adding a little bit of water for easy cooking if necessary.
3. Season with salt, then add the herbs, zucchini and eggplant. Cook until the vegetables are soft.
4. Add cheese and stir until it has melted. Cook the veggie wurstel according the guidelines on the packet. Once cooked cut into cubes.
5. Heat the bread in the oven for about 10 minutes at 180°C (350°F/gas 4).
6. Stuff the bread with the vegetables and wurstel and serve immediately.

# CHOCOLATE FONDUE WITH SEASONAL FRUIT

*Fonduta di cioccolato con frutta di stagione*

This is one of those pleasures that I love when, in early spring, the weather gives an ideal day to enjoy a fondue with excellent raw chocolate and seasonal fruit.

The fondue is not 'just' melted chocolate but is a praise of the flavor of chocolate. So choose the best quality chocolate you can.

## Ingredients

300 g (11 oz) raw dark chocolate, 70%
50 g (2 oz) butter
2 persimmons, not too ripe
3 kiwis
Juice of 1 lemon

**Serves 4**

## Method

1. Break the chocolate into small cubes and melt over a low heat in the fondue pot or a double bottomed pan. Add butter and mix until it forms a smooth cream.
2. Cut the persimmons into slices or cubes according to your taste. Peel and slice the kiwis.
3. Dip the fruit in the fondue and serve hot.

# BANANA TIRAMISU CUPS

*Tiramisu di banane in coppette*

In Italian the word 'Tiramisu', associated with one of the most popular desserts in the world, means 'feel better', to give pleasure. If such sweetness and wellness are enclosed in a glass, rich with fruit and creamy yogurt, gluttony is even more enjoyable.

Ideal served after a meal, it is also particularly suitable for children's snacks.

## Ingredients

100 g (3½ oz) brown rice flour
2 tbsp raw brown sugar
50 g (2 oz) cold butter, cut into cubes
2 ripe bananas
Juice of one lemon
100 g (3½ oz) rice yogurt
100 g (3½ oz) brown rice cream
2 tbsp sugar-free granola

**Serves 4**

## Method

1. Mix the flour, sugar and butter and knead quickly to form a sandy dough.
2. Crumble the dough, more or less coarsely, according to the tastes and bake at 180°C (350°C/ gas 4) for 10 minutes.
3. In a blender, place one banana with the lemon juice. Add the yogurt, rice cream and blend until frothy.
4. Arrange the banana mix in the bottom of a glass, cover with the crumble and a layer of granola. Repeat the layers until the glass is full.
5. Decorate with the second banana cut into slices and top with a sprinkling of granola.

# COCONUT CAKES

*Tortine al cocco*

These small cakes are made with coconut flour, obtained from the pulp of fresh coconuts (not flaked). Coconut flour is a gluten-free product, rich in fiber and taste. It makes the cakes very soft and fragrant. With its freshness and fragrance it is an ode to summer, so I love to prepare these cakes in spring, when the warm weather starts to arrive.

## Ingredients

2 large eggs
Pinch of sea salt
75 g (3 oz) coconut sugar
100 ml (3 ½ oz) coconut milk
Extra virgin olive oil, to taste
200 g (7 oz) organic white Kamut or Farro flour, sifted
100 g (3 ½ oz) organic coconut flour, sifted
1 tsp organic baking powder
Pinch of ground cinnamon
50 g (2 oz) coconut flakes

**Makes 6–8 (depending on the size of the molds)**

## Method

1. Preheat oven to 180°C (350°F/gas 4).
2. Beat eggs with a pinch of salt. Add the coconut sugar, coconut milk, extra virgin olive oil and stir until mixture is frothy. Add the flours sifted with baking powder and cinnamon.
3. Pour the dough into individual portions in a muffin tray or individual tins, covered with parchment paper. Garnish with grated coconut and bake for 10-15 minutes.

# WHITE CUPS

*Coppa bianca*

---

Not only intended as an afternoon snack, this is a very fresh and refined dessert perfect to serve after a meal.

I love to prepare these cups at the end of spring, when I go to visit my dear friends in the Trentino Region (in northern Italy). From our long walks in the woods we return home with a precious basket of wild berries that we use for jams, tarts and simple but effective sweets such as this.

## Ingredients

2 bananas
Juice of 1 lemon
400 g (14 oz) plain yogurt
250 g (9 oz) wild berries

**Serves 4**

## Method

1. Peel two bananas, cut into slices and drizzle with lemon juice.
2. In a bowl, arrange the bananas, add the yogurt and stir to mix the ingredients well.
3. Wash and rinse the berries, dry. Transfer half of the yogurt and banana into tall glasses and alternate with a layer of berries.
4. Decorate the top with berries. Keep refrigerated until ready to serve.

# STRAWBERRY AND MINT JAM

*Confettura di fragole e menta*

The homemade strawberry jam has a unique flavor (otherwise, as with all shop-bought jams, it is only a mix of many refined sugars). Spread on a slice of toast it is a delicious option for breakfast or a snack. It also makes a good filling in pies.

## Ingredients

500 g (17 oz) organic
   strawberries
Juice of one lemon
100 g (3½ oz) raw brown
   sugar
Sprig of mint

**Serves 4–6**

## Method

1. Wash and slice the strawberries. Pour them in a large pot, adding the lemon juice and sugar.
2. Simmer, stirring the mixture from time to time, until you have achieved the desired consistency (usually no more than 30 minutes).
3. Remove from heat, add the mint leaves (washed and dried), cook for about 10 minutes, then take them out.

# VEG CHOCOLATE CUPS

*Coppe veg al cioccolato*

This gluten and dairy free recipe is like a match made in heaven for those who love natural sweets. The rice cream has a creamy texture and a natural sweetness.

I usually prepare this recipe with malt or honey. If you are not used to only slightly sweet flavors, you can use raw brown sugar as proposed in this recipe.

## Ingredients

100 g (3½ oz) natural tofu
100 g (3½ oz) raw dark chocolate 80%
1 tbsp raw cocoa powder
100 g (3½ oz) raw brown sugar
50 g (2 oz) rice milk
100 g (3½ oz) sugar free muesli (or granola)
150 g (5 oz) rice whipped cream

**Serves 2**

## Method

1. Drain the tofu and crumble it.
2. In a blender, place the tofu, chocolate, cocoa powder, raw sugar, rice milk and mix until the dough is like a paste.
3. Pour the tofu cream into a glass, layering with sugar-free muesli (or granola) and rice whipped cream.

# SUMMER

# ARRABBIATA PASTA
*Pasta all'arrabbiata*

Pasta *all'arrabbiata* (angry pasta), so named because it is a very hot sauce. It is a Roman pasta dish that contains all the features typical of the Mediterranean cuisine.

This is one of those recipes, with few ingredients and a strong flavor that, in summer,I love to cook almost every day with tomatoes from my garden. The fresh tomato is the crucial ingredient, if they are not of high quality, the recipe will never be a masterpiece. Chili and garlic must have a balance that gives the pasta its typical taste, and the name.

## Ingredients

Extra virgin olive oil, to
   taste
Chili powder, to taste
1 clove garlic
400 g (14 oz) tomato pulp
Sea salt to taste
2 tbsp chopped parsley
320 g (11¼ oz) short
   pasta

**Serves 4**

## Method

1. In a pan, heat the oil, add the chili, chopped garlic and cook until brown.
2. Add the tomato pulp, salt and cook until thick.
3. Cook the pasta until al dente in boiling salted water. Drain the pasta and mix with the sauce. Add the parsley and stir.
4. Serve hot.

# BAKED EGGPLANT (AUBERGINE)

*Melanzane al forno*

---

As a child, baked eggplant (aubergine) was the Sunday dish and, for this reason, was among my favorite meals.

It is a simple recipe with all the flavor and nutrition of one of the most versatile vegetables. Great when freshly cooked, baked eggplant is also ideal as a cold side dish or filling for a sandwich. You can replace Pecorino cheese with other hard cheese and add the tomato pulp between the layers.

## Ingredients

3 spring onions
  (scallions)
4 eggplants (aubergines)
Extra virgin olive, to taste
100 g (3½ oz)
  breadcrumbs to taste
100 g (3 ½ oz) pecorino
  cheese, grated, to taste
A handful of sun-dried
  tomatoes

**Serves 4–6**

## Method

1. Wash and dry the spring onions, cut into thin slices and set aside.
2. Peel the eggplants and let them soak in salted water for 20 minutes.
3. Mix the breadcrumbs and pecorino cheese together in a bowl.
4. Cut the eggplants into thick slices and dip them first in oil, then in the breadcrumb and pecorino cheese mixture.
5. Oil a baking dish and arrange the eggplant in layers, overlapping with the diced spring onions.
6. Cover with a handful of sun-dried tomatoes.
7. Bake at 180°C (350°F/gas 4) for 30 minutes.

# BAKED OVEN ANELLINI
*Anellini al forno*

*Anellini al forno* is a typical Sicilian dish, usually made with meat sauce. I prefer to prepare this delicious meal with a more healthful and sustainable meatless twist.

When in season, this dish is perfect with eggplant (aubergine) or zucchini (courgette), but during the winter months you can make it with white sauce (béchamelle), broccoli, cauliflower or other available vegetables.

## Ingredients

2 eggplants (aubergines), soaked and dried
Extra virgin olive oil, to taste
1 clove garlic
500 g (17 oz) tomato puree
Sea salt, to taste
1 tsp raw brown sugar
3 basil leaves
320 g (11¼ oz) anellini pasta

**Serves 4**

## Method

1. Preheat the oven to 180°C (350°F/gas 4).
2. Wash and slice the eggplant and let it rest in salted water for 30 minutes.
3. Remove the eggplant and let the slices dry on paper towels.
4. Heat the olive oil in a frying pan and fry the eggplant. Remove and place on cheese cloth to drain the oil.
5. In another pan, heat the oil, then brown the garlic for 5 minutes.
6. Remove the garlic, pour in the tomato sauce and season with salt. Add the basil leaves and brown sugar to remove the acidity, and simmer until the sauce is reduced.
7. Cook the pasta until al dente, in boiling salted water.
8. Arrange the eggplant in a pan, covering all sides of the pan.
9. Once cooked and drained, mix the pasta with half of the sauce, then pour a layer of pasta and a layer of tomato sauce over the first layer of eggplant.
10. Continue with a second layer of pasta to almost fill the pan. Cover with eggplant and a layer of tomato sauce.
11. Bake in oven at 180°C (350°F/gas 4) for 30 minutes. Serve warm.

# CAPRESE PASTA
*Pasta alla caprese*

In summer, on a real Italian table, tomatoes are everywhere. The variety can be discussed (everyone has their own preferences) but the quality, never. At the market or from the greengrocer, Italians carefully choose their tomatoes as they want them fresh, juicy and ripe at the right point to prepare the perfect dish (whether it be for a classic sauce – sugo – or a salad).

Of course, for one of the most famous Italian salads, the tomatoes must be excellent, especially if served with pasta. They should be 'crisp' and juicy to perfection.

A good quality pasta, made from durum wheat, will ensure a perfect al dente cooking, avoiding the unpleasant 'rubbery' effect, typical of overcooked pasta or of pasta of poor quality.

## Ingredients

2 mozzarella cheeses, made from buffalo milk (or cherry mozzarella)
2 tomatoes
Pinch of sea salt
Extra virgin olive oil, to taste
Fresh basil leaves
320 g (11 ¼ oz) penne (or other short pasta)

**Serves 4**

## Method

1. Slice the mozzarella and tomatoes (which have been washed and dried).
2. Add a pinch of salt and drizzle with extra virgin olive oil.
3. Sprinkle with fresh basil leaves.
4. Cook the penne until al dente, in boiling salted water, and season with the Caprese salad.

# CHERRY MOZZARELLA SALAD
*Insalata di mozzarelline*

Cherry mozzarella balls are elegant, perfect for single servings and ideal for any type of salad.

   This can also be a main dish, especially on hot days, when we have little desire for rich dishes but we can't give up essential nutrients for the body. Or, alternatively, it can also be served as appetizer in small glass cups.

## Ingredients

10 lettuce leaves
10 cherry tomatoes
10 pitted olives
3 tbsp balsamic vinegar
5 tbsp extra virgin olive
   oil
Juice of a large lemon
1 tablespoon chopped
   parsley
15 cherry mozzarella
   balls
5 basil leaves
4 slices rustic bread, cut
   into cubes

**Serves 4**

## Method

1. Wash, clean, dry and chop the lettuce. Wash, dry and split the cherry tomatoes in half.
2. Pour the vegetables in a large bowl and season with balsamic vinegar, olive oil, lemon juice and parsley. Add the olives and let stand for 10 minutes.
3. Add the cherry mozzarella and basil leaves (washed and dried).
4. Serve with warm rustic bread.

# GREEN BEANS WITH HARD BOILED EGGS AND CAPER PESTO

*Fagiolini con uova sodee pesto di capperi*

If you make this recipe without eggs it becomes a tasty and light side dish. With the addition of the eggs, it can also be served as a main dish or a casual dinner at home.

It's always helpful to remember that eggs are a valuable food only if their consumption is conscious and their quality and the production chain are organic and free range.

## Ingredients

1 tbsp capers
4 large eggs
500 g (17 oz) green beans
50 g (2 oz) breadcrumbs
4 tbsp cider vinegar
1 sprig parsley
10 mint leaves
5 pitted olives
50 g (2 oz) celery
1 tbsp breadcrumbs
50 g (2 oz) pitted green
   olives
Extra virgin olive oil, to
   taste

**Serves 4**

## Method

1. Leave the capers to soak in cold water.
2. Boil the eggs in a saucepan and after 9–10 minutes of boiling, drain and cool.
3. Clean the beans, removing the ends and cook until al dente in boiling salted water, then drain.
4. Blend the parsley, mint, olives, celery, breadcrumbs and olive oil until the mix forms a creamy pesto, to your taste.
5. Arrange the beans on a platter, cut the hard-boiled eggs in half and put them next to the beans. Pour over the caper sauce and serve.

# LUISA'S ROAST POTATOES

*Patate arrosto di Luisa*

My mother's potatoes are unique and they still remain one of my favorite comfort foods. For each of us, our mother's cuisine embodies the taste of childhood and all the beautiful moments of everyday life spent together. Some dishes, more than others, contain unique flavors, perhaps because they also relate to a specific stage of life. This simple recipe is one of those dishes I love most.

## Ingredients

500 g (17 oz) potatoes
4 onions
250 g (9 oz) tomato pulp
3 sprigs of rosemary
Sea salt and pepper, to taste
Extra virgin olive oil, to taste

**Serves 4–6**

## Method

1. Wash and dry the potatoes, remove the skin and cut into chunks. Place them on a greased baking sheet.
2. Clean and slice the onions and place them on a baking sheet.
3. Add the tomato pulp, rosemary (washed and dried), salt, pepper and olive oil to taste.
4. Bake at 180°C (350°F/gas 4) for 50 minutes.

# MEDITERRANEAN CEREAL SALAD

*Insalata di cereali Mediterranea*

Farro, rice and barley are the heroes of this rich and colorful Mediterranean-style salad. A light and healthy dish, perfect for a lunch or summer dinner. You can enrich this salad with the ingredients you love the most.

In the best supermarkets and in the fairtrade shops, these cereals are also available in practical quick-cook packets.

## Ingredients

8 ripe tomatoes
1 spring onion (scallion)
Black pitted olives, to taste
Sea salt and pepper, to taste
Balsamic vinegar, to taste
Extra virgin olive oil, to taste
100 g (3½ oz) brown rice
50 g (2 oz) pre-cooked farro
50 g (2 oz) pre-cooked barley
Fresh basil and mint leaves to taste

**Serves 2**

## Method

1. Wash and cut the tomatoes and onion and put them in a bowl.
2. Add the pitted olives and season with salt, pepper, balsamic vinegar and extra virgin olive oil to taste.
3. Cook the brown rice until al dente, in boiling salted water. In another saucepan, cook the pre-cooked farro and barley (washed and drained) in boiling salted water, according the cooking times indicated on the packet.
4. Drain the cereals and season with the salad. Garnish with the mint and basil leaves.

# PANTESCA SALAD
*Insalata Pantesca*

Before visiting Pantelleria and enjoying this delicious salad, prepared with care and love by the inhabitants of this small island in the Sicilian Archipelago, I thought this was one of many salads I was used to eating. The capers are the same ones that I use in all my recipes, the quality of my organic potatoes is always excellent, as is the rest of the ingredients. So why was the salad that I tasted in Pantelleria on a beautiful summer's day a few years ago taste so special? "Because the air and the ground here are magical" was the answer of a friend of mine who has lived there for years.

   A dish to try if you are lucky enough to visit this small paradise full of tasty food At home, the result can still be rewarding if you buy Sicilian capers in an Italian specialty food shop.

## Ingredients

20 salted capers
2 potatoes
10 black pitted olives
10 cherry tomatoes
1 red onion
Dried oregano, to taste
Sea salt, to taste
Extra virgin olive oil, to
   taste

**Serves 2**

## Method

1. Rinse the capers to remove the salt, squeeze dry and set aside.
2. Boil the potatoes in salted water. Once cooked, remove the skin and cut them into slices.
3. Wash and cut the tomatoes into two halves. Cut the onion into rings.
4. In a bowl combine all the ingredients, season with oregano, a pinch of salt and extra virgin olive oil. Allow the ingredients to combine for a little while before serving.

# PUTTANESCA PASTA
*Pasta alla Puttanesca*

---

*Penne alla puttanesca* (Whore's style pasta) is an Italian sauce, from the south of the country. The origins of the name are uncertain but some studies argue that the dish was served in a Neapolitan brothel. The bright colors of the ingredients recalled the underwear worn by escorts.

My twist is to add wholemeal Farro short pasta. You can find it in Italian food specialties stores but, failing that, you can replace it with Kamut or wholewheat pasta. The advantages of using non-refined wheat are multiple, both for the health and for the taste. The wholewheat pasta, for example, cooks better (staying al dente), and is much more digestible than an overcooked pasta.

## Ingredients

300 g (11 oz) wholemeal Farro short pasta
Extra virgin olive oil, to taste
1 clove of garlic
500 g (17 oz) tomato pulp
50 g (2 oz) pitted black and white olives
1 tablespoon capers
Sea salt and pepper, to taste

**Serves 4**

## Method

1. Cook the pasta until al dente, in boiling salted water.
2. In a saucepan, heat the oil, add the garlic (cleaned and chopped) and brown it.
3. Add the tomato pulp, olives and capers, mixing all the ingredients together for a few minutes.
4. Season the pasta with the sauce, adding pepper to taste. Serve immediately.

# PASTA WITH EGGPLANT SAUCE

*Pasta con salsa di melanzane*

---

In the regions of southern Italy, there are various kinds of eggplant (aubergine) that reach, once mature, the markets in the north of the country. *Parmigiana*, *Pasta alla Norma*, fried or stuffed eggplant, there are many delicious ways to cook them.

This recipe is really quite simple. Its uniqueness derives from the quality of the ingredients. The eggplants are best when they are organic, of course. Even the pasta you use is crucial. You can choose long or short pasta, according to your taste, but the important thing is that it is rough enough to hold the sauce.

## Ingredients

2 purple eggplants
  (aubergines) (or 1 large)
1 tbsp toasted hazelnuts
1 tbsp capers
1 sprig of parsley
6 tbsp extra virgin olive
  oil
Sea salt and white
  pepper, to taste
320 g (11¼ oz) pasta

**Serves 4**

## Method

1. Wash and slice the eggplant and steam for 15–20 minutes.
2. Puree the eggplant with hazelnuts, capers and parsley. Season the sauce with olive oil, a pinch of salt and white pepper.
3. Cook the pasta until al dente, in boiling salted water and then stir through the eggplant sauce (to which you can add 2–3 tablespoons of cooking water if it needs thinning out).

# PASTA WITH TOMATO SAUCE

*Pasta al sugo di pomodoro*

In Italy, pasta with tomato sauce and Parmigiano cheese is a dish of excellence. The key or secret to master is to always have the best tomato sauce. The sauce should always be thick enough to just stick to the pasta without being runny or slipping through the shapes.

   I made this recipe with Sicilian cherry tomato pulp but you can also use the San Marzano variety. Sicilian cherry tomatoes have a unique taste from the Mediterranean climate which provides the best growing and maturing conditions.

## Ingredients

1 clove of garlic
500 g (17 oz) tomato pulp
   (from cherry or San
   Marzano tomatoes)
Extra virgin olive oil, to
   taste
Sea salt, to taste
320 g (11 ¼ oz) short or
   long, high quality Italian
   pasta
100 g (3½ oz) Parmigiano
   cheese

**Serves 4**

## Method

1. Brown the garlic in extra virgin olive oil. Remove it and cook the tomato pulp until the sauce is smooth (about 15 minutes).
2. When the tomato is cooked, add extra virgin olive oil to taste and salt.
3. Cook the pasta in boiling salted water until al dente. When the pasta is cooked, add the tomato sauce and stir through.
4. Transfer the mixture into a serving dish and garnish with a generous sprinkling of Parmigiano cheese. Serve warm.

# REGINELLE PASTA WITH SUN-DRIED TOMATO PESTO

*Reginelle al pesto di pomodori secchi*

---

Sun-dried tomatoes are a very popular preserve in south Italy. In late summer, these juicy vegetables are dried in the sun and then stored in oil.

There is no single recipe for this pesto but as it is an Italian tradition, many recipes vary from town to town, from family to family. You can add or delete some of the ingredients according to your taste and their availability. The result is a summer dish, fresh, simple and fast.

## Ingredients

15 sun-dried tomatoes
1 tbsp pine nuts
2 tbsp Pecorino cheese, grated
10 basil leaves
5 tbsp extra virgin olive oil
320 g (11¾ oz) pasta

**Serves 4**

## Method

1. In a blender, place the tomatoes, pine nuts, Pecorino cheese, basil leaves and oil and blend at maximum power.
2. Cook the pasta until al dente in boiling salted water, drain and stir through the pesto.

# SEITAN WITH VEGETABLES

*Seitan con verdure*

A full, tasty dish, rich in protein and vitamins. If you haven't tried Seitan (food of Eastern tradition, obtained by removing gluten from wheat flour), this recipe may be the one to start with.

Seitan, low in fat, isn't suitable for those who are intolerant to gluten. In this case, it can be substituted by tofu.

## Ingredients

3 carrots
2 zucchini (courgettes)
75 g (3 oz) green beans
1 onion
3 tbsp extra virgin olive oil
200 g (7 oz) Seitan burger
10 pitted olives
1 red capsicum (bell pepper)
Pinch of sea salt

**Serves 2**

## Method

1. Wash the carrots, zucchini and green beans, roughly chop and steam cook them together until al dente. Once cooked, let cool and cut into cubes.
2. Peel and cut the onion and brown it in 3 tablespoons of olive oil. After 5 minutes, add the sliced Seitan and cook for 5–8 minutes.
3. Remove the Seitan from the pan, add the red capsicum, cut into strips or cubes. Add salt and cook for 10 minutes.
4. Add the steamed vegetables and cook for 5 minutes in the pan. Add the Seitan, mix well and serve immediately.

# FARFALLE WITH BASIL TOFU
*Farfalle con tofu al basilico*

Complex carbohydrates and vegetable protein become a delicious combination in this simple pasta salad dish.

You can find basil tofu (or tomato or spicy) in organic stores or in the best supermarkets. Otherwise, simply mix the tofu with natural basil (or other herbs to your liking), finely chopped, to create a fragrant and tasty dressing.

## Ingredients

200 g (2 oz) basil tofu
Extra virgin olive oil, to taste
Sea salt and white pepper, to taste
320 g (11 ¼ oz) Farfalle or other short pasta

**Serves 4**

## Method

1. Cut the tofu into cubes and sauté in a pan, with two tablespoons of extra virgin olive oil, for 3–4 minutes. Season with salt and pepper.
2. Cook the Farfalle until al dente, in boiling salted water. Drain the pasta, add the tofu and extra virgin olive oil.

# SWEET AND SOUR PEPPER PASTA

*Pasta con peperoni in agrodolce*

---

Sweet and sour peppers reveal all the colors and flavors of Sicilian vegetables. They are part of an ancient Arab tradition. In Sicily, sweet and sour cooking (*agrodolce*) changes from area to area. Some like to add breadcrumbs, some pine nuts and more.

  Sicilian food has its own personality, like this delicious recipe. Sweet and sour peppers have a unique bittersweet taste and can be served as an appetizer or a side-dish.

## Ingredients

2 onions
4 capsicums (bell
   peppers)
Extra virgin olive oil, to
   taste
Sea salt, to taste
4 tbsp light brown sugar
80 ml (3 fl oz) apple cider
   vinegar
320 g (11¼ oz) penne or
   other short pasta

**Serves 4**

## Method

1. Chop the onions finely and steam cook them.
2. Meanwhile, cook the capsicums in the oven at 180°C (350°F/gas 4) for 25–30 minutes, until they are soft.
3. Once cooked, remove the skin of the capsicums.
4. In a large skillet, pour the onions, extra virgin olive oil, capsicums (peeled and cut into strips) salt, brown sugar and apple cider vinegar.
5. Stir over a high heat and add some capers.
6. Cook the penne until al dente, in boiling salted water, and pour over the capsicum mixture. Serve cold.

# TAGLIATELLE WITH GREEN PESTO

*Tagliatelle al pesto verde*

Not the classic pesto but a completely vegan version for anyone who does not eat cheese, or is intolerant, or for those who while loving the traditional Italian pesto love to experiment with tasty alternatives.

This recipe is prepared with real Genoese basil and creamy tofu instead of Parmigiano and Pecorino cheese. You can add garlic if you like a more pungent flavor and replace the walnuts with almonds. For this type of sauce, tagliatelle, made with durum wheat flour, is the right choice because it holds the sauce well.

## Ingredients

20 basil leaves
100 g (3½ oz) creamy tofu
7 tbsp extra virgin olive
  oil, to taste
10 walnuts
2 tbsp water
Pinch of sea salt
320 g (11¼ oz) tagliatelle
  pasta

**Serves 4**

## Method

1. Wash and dry the basil. Drain the tofu and cut into cubes.
2. Pour the basil, tofu and the rest of the ingredients into a blender. Blend at maximum power for no more than 2 minutes, otherwise the pesto blackens. If the texture looks too dense, dilute with another tablespoon of oil or water, adjusting as necessary.
3. Cook the pasta until al dente, in boiling salted water. Drain and season with pesto. Serve immediately.

# WHOLEWHEAT SPAGHETTI PIE
*Pasticcio di spaghetti integrali*

This is one of those time saving dishes, essential in summer. Prepared the day before, it tastes even better after sitting and is perfect to be enjoyed after returning from a day at the beach or as a single dish at a picnic.

## Ingredients

1 small onion
Extra virgin olive oil, to taste
200 g (7 oz) Pachino cherry tomatoes
Pinch of sea salt
Pepper, to taste
320 g (11¼ oz) wholewheat spaghetti
1 sheet puff pastry
100 g (3½ oz) mozzarella

**Serves 4–6**

## Method

1. Cut the onion finely and then brown in a nonstick frying pan. Cut the tomatoes in half and add them to the onion, cooking for about 10 minutes.
2. Add sea salt and pepper to season.
3. Cook the spaghetti until al dente, in boiling salted water. Drain and stir through the tomatoes.
4. Roll out the pastry on a baking sheet greased or covered with parchment paper. Place the spaghetti with the sauce and diced mozzarella in the center of the pastry leaving a border around the edge.
5. Bake, in a preheated oven, at 180°C (350°F/gas 4) for 20 minutes or until the pastry is golden.

# ZUCCHINI BAKED FRITTATA

*Frittata al forno di zucchine*

This frittata is beautiful and, above all, good for you. It is colorful and perfect for brunch or a light casual dinner with friends, also lovely eaten cold and diced.

## Ingredients

2 large zucchini
  (courgettes)
Extra virgin olive oil, to
  taste
1 clove garlic
Pinch of sea salt
White pepper, to taste
4 large eggs
2 tbsp Parmigiano
  cheese
3 tbsp rice milk (or
  organic cow milk)
1 tbsp brown rice flour

**Serves 2**

## Method

1. Wash the zucchini and cut into rounds (scrape the skin if they are not organic). Pour the zucchini into an oiled pan, add a clove of garlic, salt and pepper and brown. Once cooked, remove the garlic.
2. Beat the eggs, add the Parmigiano cheese, rice milk and flour. Add the zucchini and gently mix the ingredients.
3. Cover a baking sheet with parchment paper and pour in the omelette.
4. Bake at 180°C (350°F/gas 4) for 15–20 minutes. Serve while still hot.

# APRICOT CAKE
*Torta di albicocche*

In summer, with apricots collected from the garden of close friends, I make this delicious and simple cake. Perfect for an after meal treat, or served with iced tea on an afternoon summer break.

The apricots must be very ripe so that, when cooked in the oven, they take on the texture of homemade jam.

## Ingredients

1 tbsp raw honey plus 3 tbsp extra

250 g (9 oz) ripe apricots

2 large eggs

Pinch of sea salt

200 g (7 oz) whole wheat Farro flour, sifted (or wholewheat flour)

2 tsp organic baking powder

50 g (2 oz) breadcrumbs

75 g (3 oz) extra virgin olive oil

**Serves 6–8**

## Method

1. Preheat the oven to 180°C (350°F/gas 4).
2. In a saucepan, melt 1 tbsp of honey. Pour it into a baking tin (or even better, mini molds with removable bottoms – 10 cm (4 in) in size) and spread well.
3. Wash and dry the apricots. Cut them in half, remove the stone and cut into cubes.
4. Beat the eggs with 3 tablespoons of honey and a pinch of salt.
5. Add the sifted flour with the baking powder and breadcrumbs.
6. Bake the mixture for 30 minutes.
7. Allow to cool, flip the cake with the help of a knife (to pass under the mold) and serve.

# BLACKBERRY AND BLUEBERRY CAKE
*Torta di more e mirtilli*

---

When I was a child, after a whole summer at the beach, my parents used to end the holidays with a week in the mountains where, they said, we girls would breath in the good air that would strengthen us for the winter. In those weeks, I also remember picking blackberries and blueberries and the sweets we prepared with them.

This cake is a classic that I love to make without sugar and refined flour.

## Ingredients

2 large eggs
50 g (2 oz) raw coconut
   sugar
Pinch of sea salt
Warm organic milk
Pinch of vanilla
   "bourbon" powder
50 g (2 oz) almond flour
200 g (7 oz) wholewheat
   flour, sifted
15 g (½ oz) organic
   baking powder
50 g (2 oz) blackberry
100 g (3 ½ oz) blueberries

**Serves 8–10**

## Method

1. Preheat the oven to 180°C (350°F/gas 4).
2. Beat the egg whites and set aside.
3. In a bowl, combine the coconut sugar and the egg yolks and whisk until creamy and foamy. Add the pinch of salt, milk, vanilla, almond flour and wholewheat flour sifted with baking powder.
4. Stir quickly to form a dough.
5. Add the egg whites and stir gently from bottom to top.
6. Pour in the blackberries and blueberries (washed and dried), and stir gently.
7. Pour the dough into a loaf tin, (25 cm long, 13 cm wide, 8 cm high) lined with parchment paper. Bake for 40 minutes.

# STRAWBERRIES AND CREAM

*Fragole e panna*

Until a few years ago, I believed that cultivating strawberries in the garden was too great an effort, compared to the benefits obtained. Strawberries are very delicate, they need attention, especially because the birds are the first beneficiaries of these juicy fruits. But, driven by the enthusiasm of my father, a supporter of self-production, I started to grow strawberries in pots. After a disappointing first year, the experience and perseverance paid off and, today, while wanting to maintain a limited production, we have strawberries throughout the summer. Now that I have rediscovered the true flavor of strawberries without pesticides, I only need a simple bowl with fresh cream to best enjoy these delicious fruits.

## Ingredients

250 g (9 oz) fresh
   whipping cream
10 organic strawberries
Juice of 1 lemon

**Serves 2**

## Method

1. Whip the cream and put it in the fridge.
2. Wash the strawberries and sprinkle with lemon juice.
3. Layer the strawberries and cream in a glass and serve immediately.

# STRAWBERRY CAKES

*Tortine di fragole*

I do not like elaborate desserts, especially in summer. This is a very simple and quick tart to prepare. For the success of the raw pastry is essential to use Medjoul dates because they are very soft and creamy. Of course, you can vary the combination of jam and fruit to your liking. In summer, peach jam and strawberries is one of my favorite combinations.

## Ingredients

100 g (3½ oz) almond flour
100 g (3½ oz) toasted hazelnuts flour
50 g (2 oz) Medjoul dates
1 tbsp raw honey
200 g (7 oz) sugar free peach jam
200 g (7 oz) strawberries, washed and dried

**Makes 4**

## Method

1. In a blender, mix the almond and hazelnuts flours with the dates and honey. Place the mixture into molds for tartlets and let harden in the refrigerator for about 15 minutes.
2. Bake, in a preheated oven at 180°C (350°F/gas4) for 10 minutes.
3. Spread the peach jam over the top. Place the strawberries over the layer of jam and serve.

# SUMMER MACEDONIA OR FRUIT SALAD

*Macedonia estiva o insalata di frutta*

In Italy, we call fruit salad *Macedonia*. The etymology of the name seems to have originated in France and means 'mixture of things'. Fruit salad is made with fresh seasonal fruit, lemon and, if desired, liqueur (but not when serving to children).

## Ingredients

3 ripe peaches
4 ripe apricots
15 strawberries
3 ripe prunes
2 slices melon
Juice of 1 lemon
3 tbsp Marsala dessert
 wine or rum
A sprig of mint leaves

**Serves 2**

## Method

1. Wash and cut the fruit and drizzle with lemon juice. Place the fruit in a dish or in a bowl.
2. Pour the wine over the fruit dessert and mix. Garnish with mint leaves. Keep refrigerated until ready to serve.

# YOGURT APRICOT CUP

*Coppa di yogurt e albicocche*

---

The beauty of this recipe is its simple elegance and delicate taste. In summer, yogurt cups with fruit are a fresh idea for a tasty but light snack, ideal as a dessert. Ripe fruit makes all the difference and has a much sweeter taste.

## Ingredients

5 ripe apricots
2 tbsp rice malt
3 Savoiardi cookies
125 g (4½ oz) plain yogurt
Chocolate chips or
    chopped nuts, to
    garnish

**Serves 2**

## Method

1. Wash the apricots, cut into cubes and mix with 1 tablespoon of rice malt.
2. In two glasses, a first layer of apricot cubes at the bottom.
3. Mix the yogurt with 1 tablespoon of rice malt. Beat the yogurt with a whisk until the mixture is creamy and pour a layer over the apricots.
4. Crumble the Savoiardi cookies over the yogurt and continue by pouring over another layer of yogurt.
5. Add a final layer of apricots and if desired, decorate with chocolate chips or chopped nuts.

# Acknowledgments

A special thanks to Diane Ward at New Holland Publishers who argues with passion for all my books and always has the right word to answer my every question.

Many thanks to Anna Brett for the excellent editing skills, directions and insight.

Thanks to the great team at New Holland Publishers, able to create beautiful books with refined and unmistakable style. In particular, thanks to Fiona Shultz, Lucia Donnelly, Jessica McNamara, Lorena Susak, Olga Dementiev and James Mills-Hicks.

Thanks from my heart to my essential crew: Piero Pardini, Giuseppe Giustolisi and Alfio Scuderi.

To my family, to be always.

To my readers, the life blood of every writer.

# About the author

I was born and raised in Italy, surrounded by the strong, intense colors and flavors of Sicily. My mother and my father passed down their love for travel, food and a passion for cooking and organic sustainable food. Before I was a food writer, I worked as adjunct professor of Spanish Language at the University. In the context of academic research, I published essays on the Spanish-American narrative in national and international Academic Journals. As freelance journalist I wrote about book reviews and tennis. Food was the subject I thought about most, though, so, inspired by

family recipes, and valuable Italian culinary heritage, I moved into writing about my experiences and studies on the subject.

Sustainability, seasonality and selection of raw materials (as much as possible local, organic and unrefined) are the basis of my food philosophy. My literary education (PhD in Iberian and Ibero-American Languages and Literatures) is the essential ingredient for a methodological approach to food writing. I believe in the value of home cooking as an instrument of culture, knowledge and education. Knowing the ingredients, their seasonality and origin, means to cook in a conscious way. I love Italian food because it is simple, colorful, with a rich selection of valuable raw materials that vary from north to south of the country. Simplicity is a privilege that Italian women always grow in the kitchen. Through food writing I love to describe this simplicity, which is also the key to my philosophy of life. My stories and recipes appear in some International food magazines. With New Holland Publishers I have published *Panini: The Simple Tastes of Italian Style Bread* and *The Rustic Italian Bakery*.

# Index

First published in 2016 by New Holland Publishers Pty Ltd
London • Sydney • Auckland

The Chandlery Unit 704 50 Westminster Bridge Road London SE1 7QY United Kingdom
1/66 Gibbes Street Chatswood NSW 2067 Australia
5/39 Woodside Ave Northcote, Auckland 0627 New Zealand

www.newhollandpublishers.com

ISBN 9781742578460

Managing Director: Fiona Schultz
Publisher: Diane Ward
Project Editor: Anna Brett
Designer: Lorena Susak
Production Director: Olga Dementiev
Printer: Toppan Leefung printing Ltd (China)
10 9 8 7 6 5 4 3 2 1

Keep up with New Holland Publishers on Facebook
www.facebook.com/NewHollandPublishers

UK £16.99
US $35.00